Children Belong In Worship

A Guide to the Children's Sermon

W. Alan Smith

CBP Press
St. Louis, Missouri

Scripture quotations, unless otherwise noted, are from the Revised Standard Version of the Bible, copyrighted 1946, 1952, © 1971, 1973 by the Division of Christian Education of the National Council of the Churches of Christ in the U.S.A. and are used by permission.

Library of Congress Cataloging in Publication Data

Smith, W. Alan.
    Children belong in worship.

    1. Worship (Religious education)   2. Children's
sermons.   I. Title.
BV1522.S64   1984   251   84-5840
ISBN 0-8272-0445-0

Back cover photo by Graham Heath, courtesy of Mobile (Ala.) *Press-Register*. Cover design by Mel Lovings.

Printed in the United States of America.

To my children—past, present, and future

Contents

Preface

I first encountered the children's sermon as a novice preacher who had become enamored of what was then a relatively new fad in religious circles. These few moments with the children of the congregation seemed at the time to be a fresh attempt to include those children in the experience of worship, and I jumped into the process with an eagerness born more of emotion than of logic. I was dismayed to find that the available material on this subject was shallow and tepid, and I resolved, finally, to go my own way in developing what one colleague has called "Moments with Young Christians."

The current book is the result of nearly eight years of weekly children's sermons in a regular order of worship. It has become clear to me that the reason children's sermons become moralistic sideshows, disrupting otherwise harmless orders of worship, is the failure of those responsible for these sermons to take them seriously as sermons.

In this study, I have attempted to present a model for developing children's sermons that reflects a conscious decision on the part of the pastor and congregation to include children as fellow members of the body of Christ. This model argues that such "inclusive" children's sermons should be based on an understanding of the psychological, spiritual, and social nature of the children who participate in them, and should include images that are appropriate to the developmental levels of these children. At the same time, these "inclusive" children's sermons should respect the integrity of the Scripture controlling the thematic structure of the worship service. Children's sermons should always be moments of worship that are integral parts of the total experience of the worship of God.

This study is far from perfect. It is, however, an honest attempt to deal with what I have come to regard as a vital link in the process of incorporating children into the community of faith. I have not written a collection of children's sermons; that may be found elsewhere. Instead, I have tried to present something of the rationale that supports the inclusion of these sermons in the liturgical life of the congregation.

I am indebted to several people for what appears here. Dr. Jack L. Seymour, professor of Christian Education at Scarritt College in Nashville, ably directed the initial form of this study, a Doctor of Ministry Project for the Divinity School at Vanderbilt University. Dr. Seymour's helpful suggestions kept my work focused and provided valuable resources as well.

The yeoman's task of preparing the rough draft was performed cheerfully by our congregation's secretary, Ms. Jackie Dismukes; the exacting work of preparing the final manuscript, both for the doctoral project and for this study, was well done by Ms. Wanda Jordan. Both of them deserve a special place in heaven!

The experiential portion of my research was, of course, the children with whom I have been in sermon over these past several years. They have been members of two congregations: the First Christian Church (Disciples of Christ), Greenville, Kentucky, and the Fairhope (Alabama) Christian Church (Disciples of Christ). It is to them that I owe thanks for the impressions, feelings, and inspiration that led me to write on this subject.

And, finally, there is my family. Our six-year-old son, Nate, and his two-year-old sister, Skye, inhabit these pages in more ways than one. I have benefited from watching them grow and seeing the applicability of the various theories treated here. My wife, Dee Ann, has pushed me beyond my normal, procrastinating abilities as I have pursued the subject. Her understanding and encouragement have kept me on task. I must thank them all, for this book is about them all.

Fairhope, Alabama
January, 1984

Introduction

The Body of Christ

The apostle Paul, like all responsible preachers, made a concentrated effort to express what he understood to be the essence of the gospel in images that would communicate his own faith experience to those in a different culture and setting. Like all good communicators, he chose carefully from the available symbols in the life-world of the communities to which he wrote. Through these efforts, many of the most meaningful images of the faith have arisen. But one of the most enduring and powerful of these images selected to evangelize the Hellenistic world was his analogy of the church as the Body of Christ (Romans 12:4–8; 1 Corinthians 12:12–31; Ephesians 4:14–16).

The interrelatedness of each of the body's parts gives Paul's body image its power. The problems of working out this interrelatedness gave Schulz his humorous interpretation of the Corinthian passage and makes it speak so clearly to the function of human, particularly religious, communities. This body image communicates interdependence, mutuality, shared responsibility, and a common relatedness to the center of being, which is life itself. The church as the "body of Christ" may certainly relate such an image to itself, for it has historically sought to incorporate its "body members" into the common experience of oneness in its center of being: God as revealed and incarnated in Jesus Christ.

Paul is not alone in his attention to Christian unity, for much of the New Testament reflects this same theme. The Gospel According to John speaks of "one flock" led by "one shepherd" (John 10:16). The Letter to the Ephesians concentrates on the work of reconciliation, the grace-ful-filled reintegration of a broken, alienated world in the work of Christ, which is to be carried on in the contemporary human sphere by the

11

church. Thus, the author (a person within the Pauline tradition) states, "there is one body and one Spirit . . . one Lord, one faith, one baptism, one God and Father of us all, who is above all and through all and in all" (Ephesians 4:4–6), and then restates the "variety of gifts" theme generally connected with the body image. Second Corinthians also emphasizes the work of reconciliation in the famous passage, "All this is from God, who through Christ reconciled us to himself and gave us the ministry of reconciliation" (2 Corinthians 5:18).

But if reconciliation, the essential unity of believers, the interdependence of church members, and the common sharing of Christ's spirit within the body of Christ are moral and religious imperatives of the faith, the church in its realistic form has, in Paul's terms, fallen "short of the glory of God" (Romans 3:23). In the past several years prophetic voices have called the church to an awareness of its "sinfulness" in excluding blacks, women, the handicapped, Hispanics, and other minority groups from both active participation and direct leadership in the affairs of the church. While there are many battles still to be fought in these areas, one must assess the efforts of these voices of social consciousness positively. The church has finally begun listening to the calls for interdenominational cooperation, for racial integration at all levels of operation, for the recognition of women as ministers, as elders, as members of the diaconate, and as members of official boards of congregations. We have come, in recent years, to realize that the body of Christ might have been subordinating some of its component parts, through its policies and attitudes, to less than affirming places. This process was both scripturally indefensible and detrimental to the health of the body as a whole. We can give thanks to those ecclesiastical "radicals" for bringing the church face-to-face with its fallenness.

There is, however, much work of reconciliation left to do. I continue to experience an uncomfortable feeling about the exclusivity of the church. It is a discomfort that began in an amorphous feeling at the start of my pastoral ministry in 1976, and became stronger when my wife and I anticipated the birth of our first child the following year. While the church has certainly made great strides in recognizing and correcting past deficiencies in the interrelatedness of various visible groups within the church, one group has remained outside the inclusiveness that we contend should be constitutive of the church: children.

The Situation: An Incident from Three Perspectives

1. Nearly everyone has seen her—the cute little five-year-old blonde who attends church services with her mother. She is lively, full of energy and motion, and whispers in tones just slightly less audible than

12

the afterburner of a Boeing 747! She is in the pew, on her mother's lap, kneeling on the floor to use the pew as a desk for her artwork (drawn on the church bulletin), waving at the baldheaded man behind her and at her grandfather ("Hi, Papa!") sitting at the other end of her pew. She rustles papers, takes the hymnals out of their holders and stacks them next to her, sings the hymns she knows, listens to the preacher talk about "soteriology" and the Amarna letters, and wonders what time "snack" (meaning the Lord's Supper) comes around.

She is bored, and rightly so; the experience of worship in her congregation is one geared exclusively for adults. The various moments of worship are excessively verbal, assume a certain degree of intellectual maturity (which, if the truth were known, would probably exclude a large portion of the adult worshipers as well), and are precut, prepackaged, and prearranged to produce a neat, orderly, yet completely colorless worship experience. Of course she is bored; nothing about worship has touched her natural spontaneity, her appreciation of movement, her need to belong to a group, or her innate ability to see the fantastic in the ordinary.

2. Her mother is "steamed," and rightly so. Her daughter has distracted her from her own worship of God. She is certain the little girl's activity has upset not only the ability of her immediate neighbors to participate fully in the liturgy, but also that of the entire congregation, and even of the pastor! She has grown increasingly self-conscious about the dagger-shaped stares of the "rear-pew dwellers," and has been told (in no uncertain terms!) to "keep that baby quiet so others can enjoy their worship." She is nearly at the end of her rope, and has recently confided to her pastor that she has seriously considered staying away from worship until her daughter is "old enough to know how to behave." At the same time, she is aware of an increasing resentment of the negative attitude being expressed toward her child and other children in the congregation. "My child is no worse than others here," she says to herself, "and she has as much right to be here as anyone else!" She is steamed!

3. The congregation's patriarch is puzzled. He dearly loves seeing all those bright, shiny, cherubic children's faces in church. But he sees the fidgeting bodies, bored sighs, and uncomfortable clothing of the children, the exasperated countenances of the parents, and the disapproving stares of the elders, and he wonders: Do those sweet little children really get anything out of sitting through the worship service? They cannot really understand what is happening, and they are obviously bored to tears. He is puzzled: Should the children be in worship, or not?

13

The Problem

A number of years ago a book entitled *Excerpts From the Diaries of the Late God* decried 11:00 A.M. on Sunday morning as the "most segregated hour" of the week.[1] The author's original reference was to the white, male, Anglo-Saxon Protestant orientation of the mainline churches, but the three scenes from the same worship service presented above suggest that children, too, are systematically excluded from the experience of worship in a majority of today's churches. They are not physically barred from participation in the liturgical life of the church (as were many blacks a few years ago). Even the most adamant proponents of children "knowing their place" would not march the offending child out of the sanctuary. Nor are children excluded from worship by legislation or policy in most congregations.

Instead, children are segregated from the rest of the body of Christ, the community of faith, by such well-meaning but poorly reasoned institutions as "junior church" and church school classes being held concurrent with worship. Or, when we allow children to be in worship with the adult members of the church, we often use language, unexplained actions, and hymns that are beyond their comprehension. The attitude of fellow worshipers toward children can range from toleration, at best, to outright irritation. The cumulative effect of these attitudes is to communicate to the child that worship is "R-rated"[2]—for adults only.

Such a communication makes a mockery of the prevailing biblical image of the body of Christ. Charles R. Foster argues convincingly that *all* are children in relation to God and in what he calls the "community of faith," and then quotes John Sutcliffe in saying:

> "It is the nature of the church to be inclusive rather than exclusive." If we begin with this affirmation, it is consequently inconceivable to proclaim a God of love on the one hand, and on the other hand to erect barriers that "exclude some on the grounds of age, education or their ability to express their commitment in the formal language of the church." Whether we begin with the recognition of the commonality of our status as the children of creation or of our interdependence as members of the body of Christ, we are led to view children as no more, and no less, the children of God than the adults who care for them.[3]

The Approach: Thesis and Procedure

It is this argument that provides the general background of this book: **the church is the body of Christ, inclusive of all its parts (including children), and should communicate through its worship God's love, respect, acceptance, and care for all the** attitude, setting, understanding of the audience, content, form, and **people of God's creation.** Worship must express this orientation in its

14

images, which together communicate the gospel to members of the body of Christ. One legitimate means of communicating that message to children in worship is by the inclusion of children's sermons in the liturgy of the congregation. Such sermons should respect the integrity of worship itself, along with its governing scriptural texts, and should also respect the developmental, cognitive, and affective levels of the children involved.

We begin with an examination of the role of children within the body of Christ where it is argued, with John Westerhoff and many others, that the obvious differences between adults and children are not differences in kind but differences in degree.[4] Childhood in relation to God is a position that children share with the adults in a congregation, and is the essential unity that brings us together as Christ's body.

Those differences in degree are presented in the findings of the related fields of developmental psychology, moral development, and faith development. Only by knowing how children at various levels of development think about, relate to, and construct their worlds can we know how best to communicate the faith to them.

The children's sermon is pivotal to this study. It is a component in a worship experience that is accepting of and sensitive to children. The children's sermon should have as much thematic integrity with the worship service as a whole as children have a rightful place in the body of Christ. We present a model for creating children's sermons based on the worship's Scripture readings, which state the word being proclaimed in images and language (loosely defined) that communicate with children, while remaining appropriate to biblical interpretation and religious development.

The second major section of the study is a practicum for the model itself. Three examples of developing specific children's sermons from the lectionary texts on given Sundays are included. The process from exegesis of the texts through an evaluation of the process is described. These selected children's sermons make no claim to perfection. They are intended to deal fairly with both children and worship. These children's sermons are examples of those that have been delivered at the Fairhope (Alabama) Christian Church (Disciples of Christ) in Year C (1983) of the Disciples/Presbyterian/United Church of Christ lectionary.

I trust my endeavor will make a small contribution to the inclusion of children in the life of the church. I pray it will do so.

Chapter One

On Being Children in the Body of Christ

The gospel is for all persons, regardless of age. The church includes persons of all ages. Worship is a corporate action in which children are participants with adults. These simple statements . . . form our theological basis for including children with the worshiping congregation.[5]

With this statement David Ng and Virginia Thomas present their central thesis in the 1981 book, *Children in the Worshiping Community*. Children are, for them, as completely "members" of the church as are adults and are therefore entitled to be full participants in all areas of the church's common life. They join a growing number of highly respected, vocal, and prolific writers arguing for the fuller integration of children into the body of Christ. Yet, it is clear that the proverbial "person in the pew" still has some misgivings about this latest "liberation" movement being fostered, not surprisingly, by many of the same voices formerly arguing for civil rights, women's rights, and other human rights in and through the church.

Any discussion of the place of children within the religious community we have called the "body of Christ" appropriately begins with an examination of our understanding of the nature of children themselves. We all know of their energy, their inquisitiveness, their enthusiasm, their lack of stereotyped prejudices, their honesty, and their openness. Children display an innocence enriched by an ability to give their very beings to relationships in a way adults find difficult. Such negative traits as prejudice, distrust, and hatred seem to be far removed from the basic nature of children; children apparently must learn these as they experience the complexities of life.

One dominant attitude toward children is reflected in the well-meaning phrase, "children are the future of the church." The intent of this statement is laudable; it shows the importance of children to the church, and expresses the church's hope for its continued ministry through its children. However, the attitude underlying this statement is that children are "not yet" the church, that they are somehow incomplete, inferior creations needing, at some future time, to be brought to fruition as fully functioning human beings.

In response to this position, G. R. Beasley-Murray (quoting Gerhard Bohne) states, "The child is not 'on the way to becoming man,' but is a man in the full sense, only in the manner of childlike existence. . . . The child is important to God as a child, not merely because he will develop later into an adult." Beasley-Murray contends that our confusion of the child's place in the church is but a reflection of our general confusion about humankind's relation to God.[6]

He is undoubtedly correct in his assessment. The assignment of the child's "place" and "time" to the future reflects a "works righteousness" orientation that demands the satisfaction of a series of increasingly complex tasks on the way to "perfection," "justification," or "righteousness." And, since the developmental restrictions of children preclude their performance of some of these essential tasks in the quest for salvation (most notably the cognitive tasks), they must be assigned to the category of those not yet sufficiently "justified" for the kingdom of God.

Under the doctrine of grace, however, all of us are essentially children. One does not develop toward salvation, one is saved by the gracious act of God in the person of Jesus Christ and through the activity of the Holy Spirit in the individual. It is the unconditional nature of grace, the "I accept and redeem you, warts and all!" attitude implied in it that relates to the children of the church. Philip W. McLarty, in *The Children, Yes!: Involving Children in Our Congregation's Worship,* expresses this acceptance this way:

> . . . once we grasp the concept that it is not by merit that we are accepted but by grace alone, we begin to see that the depth of our own understanding, the maturity of our faith, the extent of our good works, the degree of our righteous thought and behavior do not qualify us for God's kingdom, **nor does the lack thereof disqualify us.** Our place is solely a matter of God's choosing.[7]

The primary rationale for delaying the inclusion of children as full members of the church seems to be their inability to understand the complex arguments of the faith. Yet, McLarty's comment would remind us that the lack of such qualities as understanding, maturity, good works, and righteous thought or behavior have little, if anything, to do with grace.

Charles Foster uses the same argument in reverse. Beginning with the doctrine of grace, Jesus' reception of children, and the psychological contributions of Erik Erikson and Carl Jung, he suggests that children are reminders that people do not need to be complete or mature to engage in acts of love and justice, or to serve in the life and mission of the church. We are **all** incomplete and immature in relation to the glory of God. Thus, he states:

> When we begin with the theological premise that all of us, despite our differences in age, are children of God, the distinctions we usually make along age lines to describe maturity must be reviewed. This is not to say that the variations in the capacities and abilities between birth and death are not important. It is to emphasize certain commonalities in the human experience throughout the life cycle.[8]

Educator John Westerhoff has been one of the most consistent proponents of the inclusion of children in the total experience of the faith community, particularly in its liturgical work. He, too, shares the view that those of us who are adults share the designation "children of God" with those who are children chronologically:

> The biblical witness is not a romantic idealization of childhood. It is, however, an affirmation that children, like adults, are fundamentally children of God. Children cry "Abba" naturally; adults must learn to say it. What unites children and mature childlike adults is that they are both dependent creatures whose life is founded on trust in God (Matthew 19:13–15; Mark 10:13–26; Luke 18:15–17). . . .
>
> The biblical tradition affirms that the status of children is equal to that of adults. A person's being, not his or her becoming, is at the heart of the Christian faith. Indeed, childlikeness is the norm for all faithful life.[9]

McLarty, Foster, and Westerhoff seem to share a common view: that the work of grace in the lives of the people of faith is one held in common by the entire community, and one which is based on our common identity as children of God.

There are three terms (two of which appear in the quotation from Westerhoff) which need interpretation at this point: "childhood," "child-like," and "childish." "Childhood" refers to that chronological period of human development that is biologically, cognitively, socially, and phys-iologically determinate. It encompasses the years between birth and the onset of puberty or, roughly, the first eleven to twelve years of a person's life. Childhood is the period of one's life in which the bulk of the knowledge one will ever possess is learned and a style of learning is formed. A child goes from complete self-absorption, through the dawn-ing realization of the existence of other selves, through an appreciation of the value of those other selves, to a sense of his or her own relation to those same selves, as reality is increasingly constructed from the world she or he experiences. And, all the while, it is the same child pictured in our three-perspective incident in the introduction—spontaneous, creative, alive, active, enthusiastic—if a bit undisciplined.

The second term is "childlike." On one level it is a simple adjective, reflecting the behavioral, emotional, and spiritual characteristics of one who possesses the same simple beauty and unspoiled relish of life as a child. We all know rather "free-spirited" adults whose zest for living, spontaneity, and wide-eyed wonder in the presence of God's continuing self-revelation evoke images of the child within us all. But, on another level, "childlike" may be seen as a metaphor for the way one committed to the Christian faith enters into the world that is presented by the entry of the Word. This must certainly have been the intent of Jesus' invitation to enter the kingdom of God "like a child." It is to "childlikeness" that Westerhoff and Foster speak. The term "childlike" refers to the ability of persons, regardless of age, intellectual maturity, or moral development, to come to the gospel with openness, celebration, and anticipation.

Jerome Berryman suggests that children may be "as naturally mystical as fish naturally know how to swim."[10] His interpretation of the parables of Jesus speaks of a literary form operating "at the edge of language," and speaks of these "naturally mystical" children as "parable-children":

> This new climate [of today's research] may even give us the permission to review Jesus' identification of children as Kingdom-entry parables. The parable-children do, indeed, seem to have profound feelings about parables which operate at the edge of language and require art and play to be expressed.[11]

For Berryman the ability to "understand" a given parable is not as important as one's ability to enter into the world of the parable, to view its story as a participant instead of a spectator, to touch it, to play with it, and to experience it as a child would a new story. Being "childlike," then, means being willing to be moved by a story because we have entered into it and made it our own story. Theologically, "childlike" people live with what Westerhoff calls "a sense of dependent openness,"[12] which allows them to participate in a shared human experience. "Childlikeness" presents one with a world unseen by the jaded eyes of the adult orientation.

> It is in their sense of the potential in the mundane that children most effectively help us see the glory of God revealed in the common and the ordinary—in a loaf of bread, the juice of the grape, the touch of a compas-

sionate hand, a hug, a flower, a friendly and oft-repeated greeting. Such are the events of the Kingdom of God. They are most readily available to those who experience life with the wide-eyed anticipation of children.[13]

Both "childhood" and "childlike" need to be distinguished from "childish." Webster's Dictionary describes "childlike" as an adjective describing a child's admirable qualities (like those just discussed), while "childish" applies to those that are less than admirable, such as peevishness, silliness, and undependability. The "childish" person is one who insists on his or her own way, is arrogant in his or her bearing toward others, is petty, selfish, and vindictive. She or he acts like a child by stubbornly folding the arms and furrowing the brow in defense of a position in an argument, without listening to the points raised by those on the other side of the debate.

Within the body of Christ, "childhood" and "childlikeness" are attributes to be celebrated; "childishness" is a characteristic to be avoided, or at least redirected, as Paul stated in 1 Corinthians 13:11. "Childhood" can, indeed, remind the community of both its future in the emerging personalities of the children themselves (who provide a congregation with a sense of hope) and of its present responsibilities and joys. Jesus' obvious appreciation of a "childlike" faith gives us a clear call to accept the contributions children can make to a congregation's self-understanding.

The orientation being suggested for life within the body of Christ is one that recognizes children as members of that body now, instead of as potential members at some unspecified time in the future. In his 1963 book, *Christian Education as Engagement,* David R. Hunter raised a number of choices Christian education (and all other forms of education, for that matter) must make. The first of these was the decision whether to emphasize the preparation of individuals for the *future* or to minister to them where they are *now*.[14] He sees the Christian religion as "fundamentally a means of encountering God now, at every age-level, in every moment of existence."[15]

God's continuing self-revelation is not age-specific, nor is it oriented toward the future alone, but it is current, is now, and is operative in the lives of the people of God's own choosing, the "children of God" who can respond to the divine initiative with self-abandon and joy, regardless of their chronological, mental, or social age.[16]

Children need to be loved for the persons of worth they are. Walter Harrelson stated these needs of children succinctly in an article in *Foundations* now twenty years old:

1) an understanding that they are loved and accepted just as they are, that they belong to their world, that they are a significant part of the human community;

21

2) an understanding of the character, structure and values of the particular community or "world" in which they live (family, church, school, geographical community), and a recognition that they participate significantly in the structure and values of this, their "world"; and,
3) an understanding of the ideas, worship, ethical ideals and customs of the religious community to which they belong, and sufficient familiarity with these in practice and participation to feel at home in the life and worship of their religious community.[17]

Children need to be intentionally included in the total life of the local manifestation of the body of Christ, but not because they are the latest in a series of minority groups to be liberated from their bonds of oppression. Rather, the argument for inclusiveness here is based on the equality inherent in God's unqualified grace, on our common existence with children as "children of God," on our shared incompleteness in relation to the glory of God, on our interrelatedness with each other in making Christ's earthly body one whole, functioning unit. Our chosenness by the grace of God gives us our unity, which Paul's "body image" expresses so powerfully. "Now you are the body of Christ and individually members of it . . ." (1 Corinthians 12:27). We can enter into that image and make it a metaphor or a "parable" for our own understanding of ourselves as the church. Can we be the body of Christ without accepting our children as significant, interdependent parts of the body? If we are true to our faith, we cannot!

Chapter Two

"And the Child Grew and Became Strong in Spirit" (Luke 1:80)

The Psychology of Human Development

One may justifiably ask the reason for the dominant attitude manifested toward children within the church: the belief that children are not yet capable of understanding the Christian faith and are therefore not yet the church. There are obvious differences in cognitive development between children and adults, and these differences greatly affect their respective abilities to conceptualize the intricacies of that faith. The crucial issue is whether the difference in conceptual sophistication between children and adults necessarily excludes children from membership in the community of faith, the body of Christ.

This second chapter presents the stage theory models of Erik Erikson, Jean Piaget, and Lawrence Kohlberg, as well as the faith-stage work of James W. Fowler. It deals with cognitive and faith development as they relate to the life of children within the body of Christ.[18] It ends with a brief assessment of the most important contributions of this psychology of human development to the subject under discussion: inclusive children's sermons.

The present focus is on a limited group of children, those between the ages of four and ten years of age, and necessarily restricts the presentation of the characteristics of personality development to the stages that fall within those age ranges. These age ranges have been

23

Stages of Human/Faith Development
(adapted from Fowler, *Stages of Faith*, p. 52)

Eras, Ages and Stages	Erikson	Piaget	Kohlberg	Fowler
Infancy (0–1½)	Basic Trust vs. Basic Mistrust (Hope)	Sensorimotor	— —	Undifferentiated Faith
Early Childhood (2–6)	Autonomy vs. Shame & Doubt (Will)	Preoperational or Intuitive		Intuitive—Projective Faith
Stage 1	Initiative vs. Guilt (Purpose)		*Preconventional Level* 1. Heteronomous Morality	
Childhood (7–12)	Industry vs. Inferiority (Competence)	Concrete Operational	2. Instrumental Exchange	Mythic-Literal Faith
Stage 2			*Conventional Level* 3. Mutual Interpersonal Relations	
Adolescence (13–21)	Identity vs. Role Confusion (Fidelity)	Formal Operational		Synthetic—Conventional Faith
Stage 3				Transition
Young Adulthood (21–35)	Intimacy vs. Isolation (Love)	— —	4. Social System and Conscience	Individuative—Reflective Faith
Stage 4			*Postconventional Principled Level* 5. Social Contract, Individual Rights	
Adulthood (35–60)	Generativity vs. Stagnation (Care)	— —		Conjunctive Faith
Stage 5				
Maturity (60–)	Integrity vs. Despair (Wisdom)	— —	6. Universal Ethical Principles	Universalizing Faith
Stage 6				

selected because the children who usually participate directly in children's sermons fall within them. The chart on page 24 presents an overview of the stage theories of Erikson, Piaget, Kohlberg, and Fowler. It shows the relation of the first two stages to the full life cycle.

Before proceeding with a discussion of the stages in which the audience for children's sermons would exist, it would be helpful to present some significant terms and essential components of the respective developmental theories. These presentations will, of necessity, be brief sketches of complex arguments.

For **Jean Piaget,** whose investigations into human development centered around the development of cognition (thinking about thinking), a particularly crucial term is "operation." As Fowler interprets Piaget, operations are "patterned acts of transformation exercised on the objects of knowing," which are generalized (a discovery in one situation may be seen as applicable in all similar situations), reversible (for example, subtraction is seen as the reverse process of addition), capable of being coordinated into an overall system (never merely existing as isolated events), and common to all persons on the same mental level or stage (universally applicable).[19]

In Piaget's thought, the human personality proceeds through a series of increasingly complex stages in pursuit of the ability to function at what he terms a "formal operational" level. It is here, at approximately the age of eleven or later (depending upon the particular relationship between the genetic and environmental factors at work in the individual), that the person is able to think abstractly and is thus able to conceptualize, universalize, and generalize. The "work" of the child prior to this "formal operational" stage is characterized as concrete and intuitive. And, while each child is viewed as an individual, for Piaget the stages are sequential, hierarchical, invariant, and universal.

Erik Erikson also presents a stage theory, in many ways similar to that developed by Piaget. Erikson's contribution to the field is a more direct examination of the impetus that moves an individual from one stage to another. Like Piaget, Erikson's stages are sequential, hierarchical, invariant, and universal. One significant term in his theory is the "epigenetic principle," which assumes a "ground plan," modeled on the development of the fetus, which both necessitates the growth of the personality toward maturity and provides a "time of ascendancy" for each part in the progressive move through the necessary stages. Thus Erikson states:

> Personality can be said to develop according to steps predetermined in the human organism's readiness to be driven toward, to be aware of, and to interact with, a widening social radius . . . .[20]

25

In his theory, each stage has its own characteristic issue, which must be addressed through the successful resolution of a major "crisis," which calls into question the basic perspective on life by which the individual has come to view reality. He makes two significant points: first, that each component item or issue is present before its time of ascendancy (and also exists after its critical time), and, secondly, that the successful resolution of the crisis occurs toward the end of a stage and signals readiness to move on to the next stage. Each move to a new stage, then, involves "a radical change in perspective."[21]

Lawrence Kohlberg has focused his theory on a cognitive, developmental examination of moral reasoning. His significant studies address the *process* of moral thinking, rather than the *content* of such thinking. Like Piaget and Erikson, Kohlberg's theory assumes a sequential, hierarchical, invariant, and universal development for the personality. His model does not begin until approximately ages four or five and consists of three levels of moral reasoning, each of which contains two stages of development and is characterized by a typical style of role-taking. For Kohlberg, a new internal cognitive reorganization is a precondition for a stage move, and a major factor in that reorganization is the adoption of "principles" that become the basic means by which the individual makes sense of the world. One of his most significant contributions to the discussion of human development is the suggestion that the individual is able to understand and be intrigued by the issues common in the next stage of development beyond one's own, while rejecting those issues of the preceding stage. Thus, like Erikson, he suggests a sense in which a person is "pulled" toward the next higher stage.

James W. Fowler has applied the stage theory of personality development to faith development. Like the first three persons treated here, Fowler presents a model of stages that is sequential, hierarchical, and invariant; however, he has not presently suggested their universality. Fowler understands faith as a relational event, rather than a possession; a "way of leaning into life."[22] "Faith is that *knowing* or *construing* by which persons or communities recognize themselves as related to the ultimate conditions of their existence."[23] Because of his intentional orientation to the issue of faith, which he sees as a combination of the affective and cognitive dimensions of a person's being, he is receptive to the inclusive view of the individual. In his view, the faith of children in the earlier stages is largely a dependent faith, which is lived out almost exclusively in relation to that of some other person or group of persons. It is only with the onset of adolescence, and the accompanying advent of Piaget's formal operational thinking, that the child begins to develop

26

his or her own beliefs about the central issues of the inherited faith of church, home, and social group.

Fowler also contributes a bit of clarity to an issue at which Erikson only hinted: that the process of moving from one stage to another requires fresh reworking of the major issues resolved in each preceding stage, a process he refers to as the "recapitulation of previous faith stages."[24] Fowler's work gives a fresh perspective from which to view the nature of children within the body of Christ, and it suggests some helpful corrections to the heavily cognitive studies of Piaget, Erikson, and Kohlberg.

Infancy (Ages 0–1½)

One of the findings of the developmental approach is that each stage seems to have a particular agenda or "life work" with which each individual must deal. That agenda that is not successfully handled within a particular stage must be dealt with at some point before any of the other, more sophisticated and complex agenda items may be successfully resolved.

The major physiological tasks of infancy center around the process of "incorporation," as the child learns to master the art of getting and holding onto things. This begins the work of bringing the hostile, outside world into one's self-absorbed sphere of influence, and thus of controlling and making sense of the world around one. Piaget's description of this period as "sensorimotor" refers to the task of establishing a controlling relationship between one's perception of objects and one's ability to manipulate those objects.

The primary psychosocial agenda items in infancy center around what Erikson has called "basic trust," which he describes as "what is commonly implied in reasonable trustfulness as far as others are concerned and a simple sense of trustworthiness as far as oneself is concerned."[25] Far from being a trivial issue in the broad scope of human personality development, the acquisition of a sense of "basic trust" is the "cornerstone of a healthy personality."[26]

This sense of basic trust of both the world around the child and of the child himself or herself becomes that upon which all other decisions are based. Basic trust provides a foundation by which the very young child might "lean into life"; it is, therefore, a crucial period in the development of a healthy faith.

Erikson contended that the healthy development of basic trust was the basis of religion itself. "Whosoever says he has religion must derive a faith from it which is transmitted to infants in the form of basic trust; whosoever claims that he does not need religion must derive such basic trust from elsewhere."[27] The ability to acquire this basic trust is not so much a cognitive process as an affective, feeling-oriented one. As the child begins to structure his or her world, the attitude of the parents, particularly of the primary caregiver, toward the child and the world around him or her becomes crucial to the way in which that world is perceived. A healthy sense of trust, communicated by an infant's parents and significant others, is vital for the formation of a healthy faith as the infant grows.[28]

Thus, this period of infancy is one of importance in the development of a healthy, mature faith, requiring that all concerned with a person's faith development be sensitive to those things that might help that person achieve a trusting, hopeful perspective on the world and on her or his place within that world. Our intuitive urge to smile at, touch, cuddle, and love the infant is one of the most significant contributions we may ever make to that child's future relationship with God, with faith, and with the church as the body of Christ. The development of a positive affective sense of basic trust is one of the most important things we may offer infants as they struggle to make sense of their environments.

Stage One—Early Childhood (Ages 2–6)

The first formal stage in the models of Kohlberg and Fowler is that of "early childhood," or roughly ages two to six: the age of preschoolers. The primary agenda item for the child in Stage 1 is that of control, and the growth of the child in this stage is a steadily increasing ability to exercise control over more and more of her or his environment.

The agenda manifests itself in the physiological sphere early in the stage, when the "incorporative" character of infancy gives way to an emphasis on elimination. Taking and getting are replaced with the conscious decision to throw away and drop those same items. Such a change in perspective is possible because of the physiological development of the muscle system and the growing sense of control over these new muscles.

These new physiological discoveries succeed in touching off the major psychosocial issue, which Erikson has identified as the struggle between "autonomy" and "shame and doubt." The successful resolution of the issues that present themselves in the early portion of this stage help to develop a sense of growing mastery over one's environment. The basic orientation of the Stage 1 child is still quite egocentric, as the child begins to sense his or her will and establish areas of her or his life in which autonomy may begin to manifest itself.

A parallel development during this period is that of language, which is a complex coordination of muscle control and control of one's environment. With the emerging ability to "name" one's environment (and thus to control it) the sense of autonomy, which has been exerting itself in successful toilet training, in the widening scope of "significant others," and in the ability to run and dance instead of walk and stand, becomes ever more established. The child's dependence upon the parents and other adults becomes less absolute as the child exercises mastery over more and more aspects of his or her life. Far from replacing basic trust as a life issue, autonomy begins to interpret the ways in which that trust is experienced as one lives in an increasingly understood and trusted world.

A portion of this developing autonomy seems to center around the ability to begin conscious decision-making. Piaget regards the character of this period as "preoperational" or intuitive, and suggests that the decisions made in Stage 1 are reactions to individual episodes and isolated events rather than the result of a careful sifting of options within the context of a grand view of the many facets of reality. It is the episodic character of children in Stage 1, the inability to make generalized connections between isolated events, that leads Piaget to call this stage preoperational.

The characteristics of children in this stage have implications for the development of faith as well. Fowler's "intuitive-projective faith" shares Piaget's assessment of the episodic character of the thought processes of children. The developing will is unable to separate fantasy from reality, the natural from the supernatural, and knowing from feeling. For Fowler, the most important single factor in this stage is the emergence of the imagination, "the ability to unify and grasp the experience-world in powerful images and as presented in stories that register the child's intuitive understandings and feelings toward the ultimate conditions of existence."[29] The child between two and six does not "reason" in a formal sense; instead, he or she connects facts, imitates actions, and reinterprets events with flights of fancy.

The increasingly complex work of expanding the boundaries of one's control over one's environment in Stage 1 is still limited by the basic dependence of children upon their parents. John Westerhoff has argued that the faith of children in this period is basically dependent in nature, and has used the term "affiliative faith" to describe it. In his view, the source of authority for such faith resides in the community and its traditions.[30]

Kohlberg's "cognitive-developmental" stages begin in the latter portion of this age grouping with his "preconventional level." Like

Westerhoff, Kohlberg sees a largely dependent relationship existing between children and the adults and institutions around them. The process of moral decision-making in this preconventional level is characterized by the need to conform to cultural rules of "good and bad" and "right and wrong" solely on the basis of the rewards or punishments that accompany those decisions. He, too, senses the inability of preschool children to generalize about the universal applicability of decisions, and contends that the major moral issue of this stage seems to be the avoidance of punishment and a deference to the authority of others.[31]

As can be seen on the chart, Kohlberg's entries are parallel to Erikson's next stage in which the identified crisis is "initiative vs. guilt." At this level, the child is becoming more purposive in his or her actions as the will becomes less a factor. In this stage the child begins to make a broader range of decisions for herself or himself, while taking a greater sense of initiative in beginning projects, solving minor problems, and bringing a sense of work to his or her play. The basic orientation of child to environment is still largely a dependent one.

The preschool, Stage 1 child is heavily involved with an emerging self-awareness, struggling to control his or her environment, and able to construct reality by stringing together logically unrelated events with an imagination that is marvelous to behold. While Stage 1 may not be operational or truly cognitive, it **is** creative. While children of this stage tend to deal only with the **content** of the faith that they are given by adults, they are also actively engaged in their own imaginative attempts to internalize this acquired faith. These early forays into faith are certainly imitative of the faith they experience from their parents and other significant adults. Yet these same children are experiencing a dependent, intuitive faith that revolves around personal feelings about the importance of that faith, trust directed toward others and oneself, and a burgeoning autonomy and self-awareness. Such a state of affairs should make those of us with responsibilities for children more conscious of our own faith and the ways we model that for our children.

Stage Two—Childhood (Ages 7–12)

With the advent of Stage 2 (ages 7–12) comes the parallel beginning of the formal schooling process. In this stage, the major agenda item appears to be the solidification of a sense of personal mastery over both the world of things and the world of interpersonal relations. The child in the elementary school period needs to develop a sense of accomplishment and to feel that his or her work is important, meaningful, and progressing at an appropriate rate. Erikson states, "As he once un-

30

tiringly strove to walk well, and to throw things well, he now wants to make things well."[32]

The ability to make things accompanies the move to what Piaget has termed the "concrete operational" stage, in which the child has progressed beyond the episodic character of thinking and has become able to make certain logical connections between cause and effect. In the early school years, the child begins to accumulate concrete facts, to add them together, and to develop the ability to plan toward a goal. Thus, a five-year-old who wishes to build an airplane knows to use some pieces of wood, nails, a hammer, and some glue. With a mental picture of what an airplane looks like and with the application of some rudimentary techniques, he or she constructs a reasonable facsimile of an airplane.

The child of this stage is at a largely transitional period. While he or she has become capable of following a process of logical progression in the thought process, such planning is almost entirely concrete in nature. Abstract ideas, such as love, faith, sin, and spirit are not grasped as easily as concrete images like God as father (or mother), the love of a shepherd for his or her flock, or other such tangible and relational images. Stage 2 children tend to be literal and very sensitive to rules and regulations.

Kohlberg also senses the development of the ability to take another person's perspective in this stage. During the childhood period, Kohlberg sees the individual moving through the final stage of the preconventional level, which he labels "instrumental exchange" and, toward the end of the period, into the first stage of the "conventional" level, which he calls "mutual interpersonal relations." In the first of these, Kohlberg presents children who are still quite hedonistic and egocentric but who are beginning to allow the needs of others to affect their decision making. The personal need for reciprocity, which Erikson and Piaget also describe for children of this age, is manifested on the moral level in the emergence of the call for fairness as the essential test of a decision's merit.[33]

The second of Kohlberg's stages in the childhood period is a time in which membership in significant groups becomes the most important single factor. Thus, conformity and loyalty to the group and its goals becomes the determining factor in many decisions made by the ten-to-twelve-year-old. As he describes this stage, the primary orientation of the individual is that of being recognized as a "good boy" or "nice girl," with pleasing others, particularly those within significant groups, the major task.

The faith of the Stage 2 child remains relatively dependent, but the child in elementary school has begun to move away from the imaginative, fantasy-filled viewpoint of early childhood and has adopted an interest in facts, personalities, and concrete examples of faith. The basically literal orientation of this stage, the growing ability to distinguish reality from fantasy, and the agenda items of personal mastery and a longing for acceptance in significant social groups combine to make this a challenging era for those who work with children. As children can begin to link together logically the episodes and events of the Christian tradition, they begin developing their own unique ways of viewing the content of faith. Their orientation toward the group, and increased sense of loyalty to goals shared by that group, make this a crucial time in the attempt to nurture children in the church.

With the shift to what Fowler describes as a "mythic-literal" faith, the images by which one would present the Christian faith must change. The child of Stage 2 needs to feel that his or her contribution to the common life of the church is an important one and needs to sense a shared responsibility for the maintenance of the faith celebrated by the body of Christ. In the process of development over these six years of life, the faith of the child becomes more concrete and literal, less imaginative and flighty, and more a matter of personal conviction. The received faith becomes his or her own faith, with an increasing appreciation of the interrelationships of characters and perspectives in the narrative art. A story becomes the most accepted means of communication with him or her. She or he begins to be able to take selected roles and project himself or herself into the story. Such "perspective-taking" is a prerequisite for the development of abstract, formal operational thinking, which reaches its ascendancy in the next stage.

If it has a major limitation, the "mythic-literal faith" may easily deteriorate into a formalized fundamentalism with an exaggerated orientation to works righteousness. The literalism, need for group membership and approval, and drive toward personal mastery characteristic of Stage 2 may produce a faith that is too rules-oriented and prone to perfectionism. These are tendencies of the stage that must be anticipated and downplayed by those given the task of directing and nurturing children in their faith pilgrimages.

The basic belief of this book is that children **can** have faith and that it is within the worshiping community that they can have faith most abundantly. Understanding the developmental levels of thinking and appropriating the content of faith will help those of us who lead in the church's experience of worship to develop ways to communicate more fully with the entire body of Christ.

In the church's work with children, we need to be able to use the contributions made by the developmental approach to children and to

32

apply those positive understandings of how children reason and process the information they receive to the methods we use in teaching, preaching, speaking, and relating to children within the body of Christ. Although children may be somewhat lacking in cognitive understanding of the faith, they make up for their deficiency in their ability to experience faith affectively and personally.

In order to best serve the children in our midst, we must begin to develop ways of presenting the essential elements of faith to them, ways which take seriously their characteristic way of thinking and appropriating information. When we can do that, the church will have begun treating children as fellow members of the body. It is to this conscious decision to do so that the remaining chapters turn.

Chapter Three

Worship, Children, and the Body of Christ

If it is within the community of the body of Christ, the church, that persons come to experience the essential inclusiveness of a shared calling to faith by God through Christ; and if children are both an integral part of that body and persons capable of experiencing the presence of God and thereby having faith; then children should be welcomed and encouraged to participate in all elements of the common life of that body's fellowship. Although children may see the various elements of faith incompletely or imperfectly, they experience both the importance of life within the faith community and the power of the symbolic structures of faith as they participate along with the adults of the congregation in the various acts characteristic of the body of Christ.

The worship of the community is one of the most symbolically and affectively pregnant acts of the body of Christ. It is in the sharing of the word through Scripture, sermon, prayer, praise, and song that the cognitive elements of faith are joined with its confessional, interior, and affective elements. However, because of the nature of the traditional approaches to Christian education, needing as they do to deal creatively with the developmental differences between the various age groups, a sense of separation, rather than integration, is fostered. Generational differences are virtually institutionalized here, making a sense of the essential unity of all members of the body of Christ difficult to maintain. Contemporary approaches to Christian education are attempting to resolve this dilemma through various efforts at "intergenerational" education. There remains, however, a sense of brokenness between the educational and liturgical lives of the church, and this sense just might exist because church schools foster segregation by age as much as worship suggests integration by grace.

It is the shared experience of worship that provides the best opportunity for the inclusion of all parts of the body of Christ. This chapter examines the nature and function of worship, and then looks specifically at children worshiping as a part of the body of Christ. This discussion, together with the ones preceding it, will lead to a treatment of the children's sermon as a method for furthering this inherent inclusion that takes place in worship.

Inclusive Worship

Worship is a communal act, shared by a gathered community, in which the participants jointly and individually give praise to God, receive and celebrate the revealed word of God in Scripture and proclamation, share their faith in public confession and in song and response, open themselves to God's leading and give thanks for grace in prayer, and participate in shared symbols, which serve as statements and signs of power in their own lives. It is a dynamic interplay of word of God and words of humanity, presence of God and the worshiper "presenting" himself or herself. It is not a performance by amateur and professional actors or musicians, not an aesthetic or "artsy" experience, but rather the assent of human being to divine Being, a celebration of God's grace, and a collective means of giving thanks to God for the blessing of life. The great Danish philosopher Sören Kierkegaard contended that in Christian worship God is the audience, the congregation the actors, and the minister the director. Kierkegaard is not only correct, but also a healthy corrective to the "production numbers," slick commercialism, and galloping egotism of many of the video-ecclesiastical superstars.

C. Ellis Nelson expresses a belief in the centrality of worship to the development of faith. He contends that in worship:

(the) gathering of believers to express their beliefs through power, song, reading and explanation of Scripture, to confess their sin, and to celebrate the sacraments is the very essence of the Christian faith . . . worship springs from levels of our being deeper than our reason. It is motivated by sentiment more powerful than our will. That is why worship communicates; it is the whole person demonstrating what faith is.[34]

All worshipers have the same access to the mysteries of God, and all are brought together by their shared response to the actions of God upon

36

them individually and collectively. Nelson suggests four major contributions the congregation as the body of Christ makes to the development of an individual's faith: a) through its worship it incubates faith; b) the fellowship of believers makes faith operational by relating words to experience, relating experience to affirmations of faith, and keeping various faith-affirmations in balance; c) the community of believers makes faith meaningful through its search of the Scriptures; and d) by confronting issues, the congregation makes the faith ethically alive.[35]

Worship is, or at least can and should be, the central enterprise of the church as community, as the body of Christ. Worship, more than any other single activity of the congregation, defines who we are as the body of Christ, because it is not solely cognitive-intellectual, nor is it purely emotive-affective. Instead, the worshiper is involved as a total person as he or she participates in the movement (standing, sitting, bowing, genuflecting, kneeling, etc.), the hearing, the responses, the sharing of Christ's body in the sacraments, and the offering of his or her own body through the giving of money during the offertory. Worship is mysterious and factual, symbolic and concrete, imaginative and pragmatic, and it is all these things simultaneously for all people. Iris Cully states, "Worship is central in the Christian community, and participation in congregational worship is one of the marks of the Christian person. The word 'liturgy' means 'common work' and suggests an act in which all present are engaged."[36]

Worship is both a cumulative experience of the significance of the faith and a distinct moment of encounter with God. In defense of the former point, Donald Miller expresses the opinion of many that the power of worship lies in its regularity, in the steady influence of common themes, shared fellowships, feelings of acceptance and love, and the relating of the word of God to personal existence on a regular basis.[37] This cumulative effect of worship is a combination of personal expectancy and openness to be influenced, the meaning which that person attaches to her or his experience in worship, and the event of worship itself.

Both a characteristic perspective and a personally experienced meaning are developed, altered, and changed significantly as the individual participates on a regular basis in the service of worship. David Ng and Virginia Thomas suggest:

> While there are many things children ignore or do not understand in a specific sermon, one thing they *can* understand is the importance of this act in the lives of the adults and the community they love and trust. This is a cumulative understanding. It does not come from one Sunday in the sanctuary.[38]

Thus, while the "revelatory moment" is certainly possible on a person's annual visit to the sanctuary of his or her choice, the internalization of the faith gained by that revelation, its application to his or her life, and to a large extent its meaning, must be worked out in a regular sharing in the tradition, current interpretation, and affective significance of faith within the faith community, the body of Christ.

The one "frame of reference" that has remained a constant source of authority, content, and revelation for the church has been the Bible. The church has been called a "people of the book" because of the central role of the Scripture in providing a means of engagement between God and the people of God. It seems appropriate in this age of the church to speak of an interaction of the sacred and the profane as the biblical witness is opened up and applied to the human condition. It is in the Scripture that we truly meet God, and it is in the centrality of the Scripture in worship that that meeting begins to have some meaning.

The Bible is that which gives structure and a strong foundation to what we experience when we worship. The biblical basis of worship provides a firm grounding for those who participate in it in the ongoing revelation of God's will throughout the history of a particular people. What could be a more cumulative experience for a community than to begin to see itself as a participant in God's self-disclosure now, in the past, and in the future? It is as the worshiper sees himself or herself in the parables, is moved by the poetry of lament, or thrills to the promises of the reign of God that she or he begins to sense the interrelatedness of persons touched by the grace of God.

The use of the lectionary as an integral part of worship reinforces the cumulative effect of regular participation in congregational worship. Ideally, the lectionary presents a connected, progressive reading of virtually the entire Bible over a three-year period, and the worshiper present on a regular basis would have engaged in at least some form of interaction with the Scripture through the hearing of the word of God in that period of time. The increasing popularity of lectionaries presents those who worship with a heightened sense of the importance of the Bible as a guide for living the Christian life and for proclaiming the Christian story. Because the five major lectionaries are at least analogous to each other, their use emphasizes the unity of the Christian message in an ecumenical sense; because they are keyed to the emphases of the seasons of the church year, their use provides a thematic organization of the experience of worship, with the witness of the biblical material as the organizing principle.

The use of the lectionary alone will not, however, promote the unification of worship around the thematic center of Scripture. The reading of assigned biblical passages must be given emphasis in a number of different ways. The congregation might be prepared for the celebration of church seasons by the publication of worship notes that interpret the season and its emphases, the significance of the liturgical colors, and the assigned lessons and sermon titles based upon them, along with encouragement of the congregation's members to read and reflect on the assigned texts prior to worship. When this is done, the worshiper is more likely to dialogue with the texts, sermons, and prayers than would one who comes to the service with less preparation.

The congregation might also consider providing pew Bibles, in the same translation as the pulpit Bible, encouraging the congregation to read the Scripture selections along with the person who reads these passages aloud. The texts should be read expressively from the lectern or pulpit, not as a public performance, but in a way that captures the excitement, drama, and feeling inherent in the texts.

The Reformation tradition has consistently emphasized the centrality of the Bible in the life of the individual Christian and within the body of Christ. Christian worship should be controlled by the central theme revealed by thorough exegesis of the lectionary readings for a given Sunday. The Scripture to be proclaimed and celebrated on the Lord's Day is the primary focus for each act of worship for that day, and for this reason, the reading of Scripture is placed near the beginning of the order of worship in our congregation. As often as is possible, the call to worship, the prayers, the responses, the hymns and choral anthem, as well as the sermon and children's sermon, are reflective of the central statement of purpose and meaning gained from the exegesis performed in preparing the proclamation of the word.

This is done for a number of reasons, the first of which has to do with the meaning of the phrase "inclusive worship." Any serious attempt to make the experience of worship inclusive of all the worshipers present needs to integrate the experience that is to bring them into a symbolic unity of fellowship. How can a service that is simply a string of unrelated episodes possibly communicate the unity of persons within the body of Christ? If we do not at least attempt to integrate the various moments of worship under a controlling theme based on the day's Scripture readings, our expressed intention of "inclusive worship" has the depth of a commercial suggesting a housewife's world is coming to an end because of "ring around the collar!" If worship is the most significant act of the community's common life, the Scripture, which speaks so clearly of God's will for us all to be a part of the realm of God, is also to be the most significant single force in the congregation's service of worship.

The children's sermon should be as much a part of the process of exegesis, of the context within the church season, and of the experience of the audience, as is the traditional sermon. It, too, needs to be integrated into the thematic structure of the worship service if it is to be communicative of the inclusiveness necessary for worship to take.

Christian worship seems to be at a particularly critical stage as shown by the growing use of such labels as liberal, conservative, intellectual, and emotional worship. It is at a critical stage because of a virtual fear of our identification with the "wrong" attitude toward worship. The enthusiasts, charismatics, and pentecostalists seem more adamant than ever in their rejection of the rational side of faith; liberals, progressivists, and mainline churches seem more nervous about joy and spontaneity in worship than ever before. If you really want to make an established, medium-sized, mainstream Protestant congregation nervous, just shout, "Praise the Lord!" or "Amen!" when the preacher makes a strong point! We seem to have lost the marriage of mind and spirit that can occur in good worship. We succumb to a paranoid detachment from the extremes of worship. And yet that marriage must be reconciled, as Amos Wilder, one of the more sensitive and creative of the recent biblical scholars indicates in this quotation:

> . . . It is in the area of liturgics that the main impasse lies today, it is at the level of imagination that the fateful issues of our world experience must first be mastered. Before the message there must be the vision, before the sermon the hymn, before the prose the poem.[39]

In the recovery of imagination, spontaneity, and trusting assent of being to Being, children might well teach us about the role of worship. It is to that subject that we shall now turn.

Children and Worship

Horace Bushnell, ever pleading the cause of children in the church, put the problem of children and worship directly to the fore: "I think I see it clearly, we do not preach well to adults because we do not learn how to preach to children."[40] Besides his advocacy of child-oriented education, Bushnell spoke supportively of children's participation in worship: "They should be formally addressed and prayed with. They should join in the hymns, especially simple ones such as those used by the Moravians."[41]

In light of Bushnell's timely claims and the previous arguments of this study, it would be well to examine the issue of children and worship by addressing two separate questions: What can worship contribute to faith development in children? What can children contribute to worship of the church?

Do Children Get Anything Out of Worship? We must essentially return to the question raised by the congregational patriarch in our introduction: Do those sweet little children really get anything out of sitting through the worship service? If we mean by that question: Do they understand everything that is going on in worship?—and define "understand" in Piaget's "operational" terms (or Goldman's cognitive view of faith)—then the answer must obviously be no. But the same answer would also be applicable to the average person in the average pew on Sunday morning, no matter what his or her age. In their faith development, many persons in the church are in Stage 3, described in the chart in Chapter Two. Much current literature calls for increased liturgical education for the congregation. William Willimon states the belief that an increased knowledge of the theological foundation of worship results in a greater appreciation of it,[42] while Iris Cully contends that all aspects of worship necessarily have a teaching function as regards the Christian faith.[43]

Thus, the common question about children's appropriation of worship and its elements is even more common than the questioners realize. Still, the developmental issue causes some reluctance. Once we, as a congregation, decide to begin allowing, even encouraging our children's participation in worship, at what age should we begin to do so?

Philip McLarty argues that even the youngest of children can "get *something* out of worship." As the infant is held snugly and proudly by his or her parents in the worship service, the variety of sights, sounds, colors, smells, and especially feelings related to worship, and especially to mother and father *in* worship, create what he believes to be lasting impressions of the value and importance of such a community celebration.[44] He may be correct; however, the majority of the impressions of worship for infants are related more directly to the basic trust being instilled by the parents' attention to her or him than to worship itself. This is not to downplay the significance of that phenomenon in any way, however, for the developmentalists have shown us that the role of the parents and the development of trust in the infant are directly related.

The major problem with this argument is that many parents, especially those entering parenthood for the first time, worry so unjustifiably that their baby's squirming, whimpering, and crying will disturb the worshipfulness of the setting that they become overanxious, defensive, and compulsive in their attempts to keep the child quiet and occupied. Thus the parents are distracted from hearing the word and responding to it; the neighboring worshipers are more distracted by the parents' obsession to entertain the child than by the child himself or herself; and the child is distracted from all those worship sights, sounds, colors, smells, and feelings by the parents' attempts to absorb all the child's attentive faculties.

There are a number of distinct advantages for the child in his or her participation in the congregation's worship. Allowing and encouraging the child to participate in the congregation's worship communicates to her or him the simple fact of his or her **acceptance** by the body of Christ. It tells that child that he or she is an important part of the body and at least an equal with the adult members of the body.

This would be an important communication to both the Stage 1 and Stage 2 child. To the child in Stage 1, this feeling of acceptance would reinforce the growing need for self-assertion and personal initiative by telling her or him, "You are important to us. We affirm you and your 'work'." To the Stage 2 child, it would address the burning issue of childhood—personal mastery—with the affirmation that what she or he was doing was both "good" and "important." Since groups are increasingly important as children develop their sense of identity and adopt moral rules, our acceptance of their participation in worship would communicate God's love and acceptance as well, and contribute greatly to later theological conceptualizations of God.

Such acceptance as a person of worth fosters the related understanding of the child's **sense of relatedness to the body of Christ.** In the earliest years of the child's life, this sense of relatedness is communicated almost exclusively through the family.

The development of the feeling of belonging, of relatedness may be extended beyond its introduction in the life of the family to the church. The church expresses the same experience of belonging, of relatedness by celebrating the child's presence in its midst through mutual participation in worship. The need to belong is not age-determinate; all humans need a sense of relatedness to others. The Scriptures teach it, and the inclusion of children can help them experience it internally, as well as hearing it intellectually. The child of Stage 2 would be particularly appreciative of such belonging.

Participation in worship with adults **helps the child experience the importance their parents and other significant adults attach to their faith and to worship itself.** As Westerhoff, Goldman, Piaget, and others have demonstrated, the faith of childhood (i.e., prior to the adolescent beginnings of "formal operational" thinking) is largely a dependent faith. Children tend to appropriate and articulate the faith of their parents, teachers, or community. Therefore, the experience of being in worship with these significant adults and seeing them being "fed" by the word of God, the fellowship, and the symbols of worship has a tremendous effect on the "frame of reference" the child will bring to the matters of faith when he or she begins developing a personal faith.[45]

Participation in worship with adults **teaches a valuable lesson about the nature of the church.** Avery and Marsh wrote a song a few years back which gave expression to a great truth of the church: "We Are the Church" has as its chorus, "I am the church; you are the church; we are the church together. All who follow Jesus, all around the world! yes, we're the church together."[46] Our sharing in worship with children communicates our interconnectedness, interrelatedness, and inter-dependence. Although the formal conceptualization of the nature of the church may have to wait until the rational processes mature and become more sophisticated, children can still experience the interdependence of church members. Through their worship they can with adults experience themselves as part of the body of Christ in ways impossible in other settings.

Participation in worship with adults **gives children the opportunity to experience the insights of Scripture as something to be celebrated, affirmed, and felt, instead of merely as facts to be learned.** The first step in believing the words of Scripture and having them influence one's faith formation is to attach significance to them. Faith is not just another academic study; its **expression** is. When a child hears history as our story, rather than his-story, experiences Scripture as personally significant and affective, knows the word as present rather than past, then Scripture begins to have significance in influencing the formation of his or her faith.

Participation in worship with adults **allows children to experience God's word and worship in a variety of forms.** Every act of worship possesses the potential of a revelatory act; if it does not, it is superfluous and should be removed from the worship service. Donald Miller says that "the moral significance of one's experience of the sacred within worship is that potentially one 'sees' things differently (to the extent that one believes there is another reality beyond that of one's everyday consciousness.)"[47]

The worship service combines movement, fellowship, music, poetry, narrative, story, proclamation, response, personal and collective prayer, reading, listening, thanksgiving, and, in my own Disciples' tradition, the weekly sharing of Christ's body and blood and our own sharing of ourselves in offering. The worship service is a varied mixture of actions and reactions, any one of which can be the avenue for a child's openness to God's presence and call. Each symbol of worship may be entered into by the child as well as any other worshiper.

Participation in worship with adults **teaches children how to be the church.** Roger and Gertrude Gobbel believe that children, like adults, learn to be the church only as they experience the church (thus, the oft-cited truism, "Children learn by doing"), and contend that worship is the best place to learn these lessons.[48] It is not enough to know what the church is; in worship, children gain what amounts to in-service training in being the church.

Participation in worship with adults **introduces children to the "old, old story."** Those affirmations of faith, biblical stories, and interpretations of both for our time and place give children a connectedness with the past, an evaluation of the present, and a promise for the future. In worship, all who are present participate symbolically and affectively in the foundations of faith laid out by the saints many years ago. The ability to reason fully has little to do with it; children who can affirm George Washington as the "father of their country" without understanding the full implications of such a statement, can likewise affirm Abraham as the "father of Israel" or God as the "creator of the universe."

Participation in worship with adults **can help children come to know that something is expected of them both as they worship and as a result of worship.**[49] They are expected to be engaged in worship, and to join the adults in translating the content and feelings of the expressed faith into action in the world. God's summons to worship must always conclude with a commission to service, and children may serve as well as be served in the church.

Westerhoff claims, "Children need to be integrated not only in the sacramental life of the community, but also in the ministry of the church in the world."[50] And in his pamphlet *Proclaiming the Word With Children,* Charles Foster argues that the stories of our faith heritage, shared with adults in congregational worship, provide "powerful resources . . . to them to cope with the ambiguities of the human experience."[51] Like adults, children can be empowered in worship to meet the problems and complex issues of life head-on, and to deal creatively with the witness of the church to those problems.

Participation in worship with adults **can help "draw" children from one stage of development to another at the appropriate time in the individual child's life.** Those who write on the developmental approach to psychology and faith agree that there is in the individual a natural "longing" toward the next higher stage of development. Challenging a person with decision making or symbolization one stage above his or her own can trigger a personal "cognitive leap." Worship chal-

44

lenges children to explore the significance of communion beyond the obviously limited nutritional value of the elements themselves. It presents children with a vision they must strive toward attaining, just as it does the adults who worship there. Worship is significant for children because it presents symbols that are at one and the same time impossible to apprehend on a cognitive level and impossible to resist on an affective level. Worship draws the child ever higher in the experience of faith, building cumulatively as it goes up the developmental ladder.

Our answer to the patriarch of our opening drama in this book must be a resounding yes! Children can certainly get something out of worship, and far more than most of us realize. If nothing else, these ten benefits of worship for children should encourage adult worshipers to become more intentional in our own worship so that we may help the children with whom we worship experience all the positive influences possible in worship.

You Mean Children *Contribute* **Something to Worship?** The question is an incredulous one, and reflects a widely felt assumption by church people that children, because of their incompleteness as persons and their faulty logic, cannot truly be expected to contribute anything more than distraction and disruption in the congregation's service of worship. But there is a significant body of literature developing, primarily in the "interface" of Christian education and worship, that has listed a number of specific contributions children can make to worship. As noted, several of these listed contributions are attitudinal, while others are more specifically functional.[52]

Children contribute a sense of **spontaneity** to the experience of congregational worship. Many worship services appear to have been constructed by the application of a cookie cutter to a consistently bland, flat dough. There are the same hymns, the same Scripture selections, the same sermons, and the same solemn faces. Children, however, experience every moment as new, fresh, and exciting. The episodic nature of thinking, which characterizes early childhood and the early school years, allows imagination to fill in the blanks left between episodes.

The spontaneity of children, the ability to unabashedly let forth with applause or cheering when the mood strikes them, is enlivening for a congregation. It forces all worshipers to loosen up their tight reign on their emotions and on their beliefs and respond to the possibility that God might do something in worship that is not contained in the denominational worship book. A spontaneous relationship to worship gives assent to the mystery, the fantasy, the symbolic nature of Christian faith, just as the ritualized form of worship gives continuity, avenues for participation, and structure to the experience. When children contribute spontaneity to worship, they contribute much.

Children contribute a sense of **receptivity** to worship. Children come to worship with a wide-eyed wonder akin to that of the shepherds of Luke's birth narrative. They are naturally open to the mysteries of faith because they have to learn to separate fact and fantasy. Charles Stinette believes that "the child divines the truth in religious symbols by intuitively entering into them long before he attempts to understand them."[53] Children come to worship expecting something to happen, and openly, eagerly participate when something does. The entire congregation could benefit from such expectant, receptive worship.

Children contribute a sense of **thanksgiving** to worship. Most children make terrible actors, because their faces are so expressive of their true emotions that they cannot adequately express emotions they do not feel. Children are thankful when we tell them, directly or indirectly, that we love, honor, and respect them as we worship with them, and their thankfulness is written all over their beaming faces, kinetic hugs, and squeals of delight. We adults have learned too well the suppression of such outward emotions, and have in the process lost our ability to say "thank you" to God, to our fellow worshipers, and often to ourselves. Children in worship with us can help us recapture some of that thankfulness.

Children contribute a sense of **simplicity** to worship. We all must plead guilty of one thing—the overintellectualization of much of our thought and speech. It is a constant struggle to rephrase theological language in more common terms in preaching and teaching. But even that "reformed" language is too abstract for children. Children think concretely, yet imaginatively. Expressions of faith by children possess that elusive quality of something simple, yet extremely profound. (Our son, on sharing communion with us in worship recently turned to me, pointed to the cup of juice and, smiling, said, "This means God loves me!" I should have recorded it, played it at the beginning of my sermon time, and dismissed church!) Bushnell said it over a century ago; Jesus said it nearly two thousand years ago; and it had probably been said for many years before that: "If . . . worship has little to do with children, it may well have nothing of significance to do with anyone else."[54] The best teachers of preaching all seem to agree that effective sermons are those for which the main purpose may be expressed in a single statement. The decision to communicate with children in worship must include the move toward simplicity in our planning, language, and action. There are few of us in ministry or as lay persons who could not benefit from the child's contribution of simplicity.

Children contribute a sense of **hope** to worship. I have already suggested the expectancy children bring to worship. But a related issue is the hope their presence and participation in worship introduces. The children themselves hope they are growing, are being accepted in the body of Christ, and will eventually become acolytes and church officers. But children also give the congregation hope in two ways: first, children give their fellow worshipers hope that the "species" will be continued, that the community will survive its members, that the body will continue to exist; and second, the presence of active children gives fellow worshipers the hope that things are getting "better" in that congregation day-by-day. Children convey a sense of congregational growth and hope for the immediate future.

Children contribute a sense of **self-giving love** to worship. Some children are extremely shy, but most children love wholeheartedly. They risk themselves in relationships with others and with God because they have not yet learned not to do so. The sense of basic trust, which Erikson saw as so crucial in the fostering of a healthy personality in children, is communicated (once learned) in the ability to risk and abandon oneself in self-giving love. A young girl, the daughter of some church members who now live away from our community, is basically shy. However, every time she sees me, she runs up and hugs my leg. She trusts me because of the relationship I have developed with her and her parents over the years, and she therefore can throw herself into her greeting of me. Children are wholehearted in their love and commitment; would that everyone in the church could make that claim.

Once we have begun to perceive the interrelatedness of contributions in worship between children and adults, the sense of our shared existence as children of God within the body of Christ becomes apparent. The grace of God calls us together as fellow members of that body in the divine self-revelation found in Scripture. The experience of self-giving love in the relationships between participating members of the body is the goal of life within the community of faith. When we can share with our children in worship and learn from them, as well as model for them the life of faith, we will live out our common status as children of God and celebrate the grace that gives us our identities.

There are many more things that could be included in both lists, but the basic message is that congregations have little justification for prohibiting children from participation in worship. Children gain enormous building blocks for a strong, healthy faith as they gather with the entire body of Christ in worship, and that worship itself will be greatly enhanced by our application of the many simple contributions children can make by their presence and participation with us as we celebrate God's presence and give thanks for the gift of grace. We are truly more completely the body of Christ as we join in worship as co-meditators with children in worship.[55]

Chapter Four

Inclusive Children's Sermons in the Worshiping Community

In 1975, my wife and I visited a small Disciples of Christ congregation on a particular Sunday morning. We noticed two things that were unusual about the service: the bulletin mentioned a "Children's Sermon," and the sanctuary had an inordinate number of children in its pews. We were both enchanted by what we saw. At the time little was being done for or with children in worship, and this was at least an attempt to include them in the worship experience. I determined at that point that I would try my hand at children's sermons when I began serving a congregation.

I had the chance to honor my determination the next year, as I began serving the First Christian Church (Disciples of Christ) in Greenville, Kentucky, in March 1976. Children's sermons were becoming popular at that time, and I began asking some fellow pastors about the best ways to begin developing some of my own. On one of my frequent trips to a bookstore, I located a number of small books of "object lessons for children" and sample children's sermons and, on the advice of these ministerial colleagues, purchased several.

I was appalled! The examples given in these books were trite, innocuous, moralistic bits of fluff. They demonstrated little theological reflection, no connection with the flow of worship, and only passing reference to Scripture. They were "cutesy" and evidently designed more to entertain the children and delight the parents than anything else. I found very little of value in those few books.

The situation has hardly improved in the last several years. Little attempt seems to have been made at developing a serious study of the theological, ecclesiological, psychological, and exegetical nature of the children's sermon within the context of worship. Three recent publications give some promise of better things to come: *Gospel-Telling: The Art and Theology of Children's Sermons* by Richard Coleman; *The Children, Yes! Involving Children in Our Congregations' Worship* by Philip W. McLarty; and an article by James A. Carr in the *Perkins Journal* entitled "The Children's Sermon: An Act of Worship for the Community of Faith."[56] Each of these provides a positive approach to the development of children's sermons, sharing the belief that children are a part of the body of Christ by virtue of the inclusive nature of God's grace.

None has dealt as fully with the nature of the faith of children and the exegetical integrity of the texts of worship as I had hoped. Carr's article, however, is more directly oriented to the careful, considered development of the sermons themselves that I present here. Carr's attempt to bring together the seemingly disparate disciplines of theology, developmental psychology, and the use of metaphoric language is particularly appreciated. This presentation hopes to take the direction signaled by Carr's article and make some significant contribution to the subject of inclusive children's sermons.

The Problem with Children's Sermons

In beginning his book, Philip McLarty relates an incident in the June 27, 1980 issue of the *Texas Methodist/United Methodist Reporter*, where an article critical of children's sermons appeared. As he reports the incident, the periodical received some four to five hundred response letters, the majority of which were supportive of the place of children's sermons in the worship of the church, prompting the devotion of an entire page of the July 25 issue of the same publication to the subject. McLarty then interviewed the editor, Spurgeon M. Dunnam, III, who indicated that a particularly "hot" issue might elicit a few dozen letters to the editor.[57] It is clear from McLarty's illustration that children's sermons are given much popular support and are invested with some sense of importance.

There are currently a number of critics of this contribution to worship, most of whom criticize children's sermons that I would also consider poor examples. There **are** problems with children's sermons, particularly if they are poorly prepared and "tacked onto" an order of worship, with no attempt at integration into the essential flow of worship. The specific criticisms leveled at children's sermons by Foster, Ng and Thomas, Willimon, and Gobbel and Gobbel are the most significant of those presented. Their objections fall into three general categories: educational considerations; theological considerations; and inclusion/exclusion considerations.

Educational Considerations

I have outlined six objections to children's sermons on educational grounds, some of which are interrelated. The first is that children's sermons tend to be overly intellectual and cognitive, either rejecting or ignoring the emotive and affective aspects of personal development. Human and faith development studies provide one of their greatest contributions to our understanding of the personality by reminding us that children are limited in their ability to process information intellectually, to think formally, until approximately the age of twelve. Willimon, for instance, states:

> . . . as we have seen from the findings of child development, the children's sermon may be the least appropriate way to reach children. Sermons are generally verbal, cognitive, intellectual activities. But children, at least through early adolescence, tend to perceive best through non-verbal, emotional, and affective means.[58]

His is a conviction shared by Ng and Thomas, and by Charles Foster as well.[59] They address children's sermons in which the preacher does not know his or her audience and has not made the effort to construct the message in such a way that it would communicate with children on their own levels of understanding. Such a misunderstanding of the nature of preaching with children is but an example of the general misunderstanding of children that seems to afflict many adults, particularly in the church.

A second common objection is technically a subtheme of that raised by Willimon above: Children's sermons (and, from his wording, sermons in general) are overly verbal.[60] He is correct in his contention that children learn more effectively through nonverbal methods of communication. Westerhoff and others have pointed out that learning takes place initially through one's feelings, and only later through facts and rules.[61] The preacher's tendency to be overly verbal and deficient in expressions of feeling and concern when dealing with children can have many sources (overly intellectual processes of training, for instance?), but the basic problem is one of the preacher's own personality. If the teacher is overly verbal with children, chances are that she or he will also succumb to the same temptation with adults.

A third criticism, raised by Ng and Thomas, is related to the first two in an almost inverse way: Children's sermons generally lack intellectual and theological integrity.[62] This objection suggests that the preacher of the children's sermon, fully aware of the lack of cognitive sophistication in the audience to be addressed, "waters down" the gospel and trivializes the message of the prophets. Even though the children who hear the sermons might be unable to process all the content of the gospel, they still need to be presented with the whole gospel!

A fourth argument against children's sermons is the suggestion that they tend to be moralistic or humanistic in their content. Indeed, many of the books of children's sermons available are filled with sermons that instruct children in what "good little boys and girls should do," instead of presenting them with the transforming power of the gospel, as noted by Ng and Thomas, Foster, Willimon, and Richard Coleman who believe that the moralistic trap is a particularly inviting one:

> Without constant vigilance it simply happens, because we do not have before us a clear-cut distinction between moralism and the Good News, between the indicative and the imperative. The indicative is the Good News that through Jesus Christ (his death and resurrection), each of us is invited into a new relationship with God. The imperative is the ethical response (both personal and social) that we make as the new creation begins to transform us. The imperative is grounded in the indicative, not vice versa.[63]

Coleman also warns of the other side of the moralistic fallacy: humanism. Such humanistic approaches to faith issues are almost as unavoidable as the moralistic ones. He states:

> If moralism is the pitfall of conservatism, then humanism is the undertow of liberalism. . . . If moralism tends to confuse the Gospel with proper conduct or proper doctrine, humanism tends to confuse the Gospel with the wisdom of the ages or parental advice.[64]

While it is probable that children and adults would find these humanistic messages entertaining and interesting, the shallowness of such "worldly wisdom" quickly shows when applied to a world where decisions tend to be made on the basis of expediency, rather than on reflection.

Foster raises the fifth objection, claiming that many children's sermons tend toward legalism. He states that they all too often, "conclude with a rule or guideline for the lives of the children rather than an affirmation about the way God acts in their lives."[65] The relationship between this argument and the preceding one is obvious; however, Foster's objection speaks more directly to the listing and following of rules that Kohlberg and Fowler have suggested are so constitutive of persons in the late stages of childhood (particularly those between the ages of ten to twelve). The "works-righteousness" orientation, heir to the Pharisaism against which Jesus railed, is enough of a temptation for the Christian searching for an easy plan of salvation without our legitimation of it in presenting a "seven-stage plan for salvation" or (from the early years of my own religious tradition) a "five-finger exercise." As the discussion of grace in the first chapter intended to show, the gospel is relational, radically person-oriented, and liberating. The communication of a legalistic frame of reference for the Christian faith to children is the opposite of the gospel's teaching of unmerited grace.

The sixth point made regarding the educational perspective is related to the first: many children's sermons tend to be too abstract and adult-oriented in their language. Willimon says, simply, "Abstract talk in children's sermons about faith, hope, and love may be interesting to adults, but it will say little to young children."[66] If a children's sermon has little to say to the children, it has little justification for inclusion in the worship service.

Theological Considerations

The second category of objections to children's sermons are those more specifically theological in orientation. They include the following:

First, Foster claims that many children's sermons make the child, rather than God the focus for the message.[67] While this may happen for a variety of reasons, the primary reason would seem to be that the attempt to make the sermon more relevant and communicative to children might easily move the focus from a statement about the actions of God in the world that affect and influence the child to a statement about the world of which the child is the center. Children up to the early adolescent years are still quite egocentric, while the gospel seems to call one toward becoming Christ-centered or God-centered. In the attempt to "hook" the child with issues that are significant in his or her life, the central role of God in personal faith may become lost in "relevance."

A second objection raised relates to our prejudice regarding the extent of knowledge a child may process. Ng and Thomas contend that the hearing of the word in Scripture and sermon are not as far beyond the scope of a child's understanding and experience as we might think:

> The dynamic process through which God confronts his people through their faithful reading of the Bible will not be understood in full until the adolescent years. But children will develop more and more respect for the Bible and confidence in it as they participate with the congregation in its regular reading.[68]

Their specific objection is the lack of orientation to a scriptural passage in a good number of children's sermons.

The third hesitancy, expressed by both Willimon and Foster, also concerns the role of scripture in the children's sermon, for both express their fear that children's sermons often manipulate biblical texts in the service of predetermined goals in the sermons themselves.[69] This eisegetical fallacy is always a temptation in the preparation of any form of proclamation and one needing to be avoided at all costs. When we begin separating any sermon from its proper scriptural context, we do damage to the integrity of the sermon, the text, and the audience.

Willimon raises the next major objection, that children's sermons tend to be unrelated to the rest of the worship.[70] I must share his concern on this point, for many of the children's sermons I have witnessed have seemed completely unattached to the rest of the service. This is a form of patronization, of the inclusion of the children's sermon out of a sense of guilt over the exclusion of children from the experience of meaningful worship. Instead of attempting to bring those same children into the fellowship of the body of Christ around the table and around the word, we insert the children's sermon as a guilt offering, with little consideration of its function in the totality of worship.

The fifth theological objection relates to the fourth: the typical children's sermon tends to place the preacher in a paternalistic relationship with the children. Foster seems to share Paulo Freire's understanding of the traditional teacher/student role as a "banking" concept of education, with the teacher doing the depositing.[71] Once we begin to reinforce the already felt "specialization" of the minister over against the child and the rest of the congregation, communicating the sense that he or she has all the answers and that the child has none, the intended goals of communicating acceptance and sharing ministries are dead.

The final theological argument against children's sermons, that they may indicate at least a subconscious admission that one's preaching has been too intellectual all along seems to me to be right on target and to need little further comment.[72] If the central point of any sermon cannot be stated in one brief uncomplicated statement, it has probably not been probed sufficiently by the preacher and will likely be expressed in language that reflects the lack of clarity that characterizes it.

Inclusion/Exclusion Considerations

The final category of objections to children's sermons deals directly with the issue of inclusion/exclusion discussed in the first chapter. There are five of these objections.

The first is expressed by Foster, who, building upon the concern over the moralistic tendency of many children's sermons feels that many of these sermons emphasize the conduct of individuals, rather than the corporate nature of the church.[73] It is difficult to maintain the tension between the natural egocentrism of children and the corporate nature of life within the body of Christ. Sermons of any type that encourage the "do-your-own-thing" orientation for the individual are an affront to the inclusive nature of the gospel of grace and to the corporate nature of the church.

It is claimed by all four of these critics of the children's sermon that the very addition of a time just for the children, in which the message will be shared with them in their own terms and images, implies that the "real sermon" is just for the adults. If it does so, it does an injustice to the process of proclamation of the word.

In a related way, the third criticism is that children's sermons communicate only with one group, the children, to the exclusion of the rest of the congregation. Willimon would add a further objection: that children's sermons tend to be exclusive even in their orientation within childhood, appealing as they do to the early elementary age group.[74] Gobbel and Gobbel feel this process isolates children from common participation with the gathered community.[75]

This process of setting children apart from the congregation destroys the inclusiveness of worship and removes children from the gathered community. Thus, the fourth objection relates to the first three in this category. Any process within the context of worship that singles out a particular group for special recognition or attention endangers the ability to remain an intentionally inclusive and whole community.

The final criticism is the impression left by Gobbel and Gobbel that children's sermons are frequently little more than pleasant interludes in the service of worship, interrupting its flow, an operation performed on the children in the presence of and for the entertainment of the adults. Adults love to see children, as we saw in the attitude of the patriarch in the introductory incident, and appreciate seeing them receiving attention. But, if the entertainment of the adults is the intent of the children's sermon, it is of no merit on its own terms, and should be scrapped.

Each of these authors joins with countless others in presenting a series of excellent suggestions of methods for including children in the liturgical life of the congregation. It is the position of this book that the inclusive children's sermon needs to be a part of a thoroughgoing attempt to so structure worship that children are included in all its ritual, meaning, and power. If we try to rely on the children's sermon alone to include children in the body of Christ, we are doomed to failure.

The Contributions of Children's Sermons

I share many of the concerns raised by these critics of children's sermons. However, I only find them to be valid criticisms of what I would consider to be poor children's sermons. They are not legitimate indictments of children's sermons as an acceptable and meaningful contribution to both the service of worship as a whole and of the children's experience of that worship. My thesis is that children's sermons, as commonly practiced in congregations, need to address more seriously their theological, ecclesiological, exegetical, liturgical, and psychological conceptual bases before they can adequately communicate the inclusive nature of the body of Christ to the children who participate.

The Educational Objection

My general response to all the objections raised is, "True, but it does not **have** to be so!" Of the educationally based criticisms of children's sermons presented, four (that they are too intellectual and cognitive, at the expense of the emotive and affective levels; that they lack intellectual and theological integrity; that they are excessively verbal; and that they are too abstract and adult in their orientation) concern an impression that children's sermons necessarily fail to take the developmental levels of children into consideration. Such sermons neglect the needs and abilities of children to process or internalize the message being conveyed while they also ignore the integrity of the word of God in the process. Indeed, poor children's sermons are guilty on both counts.

Inclusive children's sermons, however, are ones in which the preacher has taken the time and effort to know his or her audience. It is not difficult for one to find a concise outline of the developmental characteristics of the various levels of childhood. Nor is it particularly difficult to project from that information the kinds of language, images, and approaches one might use in presenting the message of the gospel to children in a way that would communicate effectively with them. The problem may be dealt with creatively if the person developing the children's sermon looks sensitively at the listening persons as developing individuals.

This "intellectual" argument against children's sermons itself commits the "intellectual fallacy" by assuming that the inability of a six-year-old to use formal logical operations excludes any appeal to reason with that child. Each person needs to be challenged by a vision somewhat beyond her or his reach. Rather than totally rejecting the use of rational categories, it would be advisable to construct the language and message of the sermon in such a way that it may be received on more than one level of meaning, depending upon the level of cognitive and theological sophistication on which the individual operates.[76] It is, for instance, conceivable that a particular congregation might have performed its task of nurture so well that its children operate at faith stages far beyond their expected development in terms of age. While it is unlikely that many congregations would find themselves in such a situation, the very possibility of such an occurrence should present a challenge to the "intellectual" argument. Is it really necessary to reject, or at least postpone the introduction of the cognitive, intellectual aspects of the faith until the ascendancy of formal operational thinking? A more appropriate approach might be the careful preparation of children's sermons that, aware of the developmental restrictions of children, combine stage-appropriate forms of communication with the affirmation of a vision of imminent growth toward a more sophisticated faith. Sensitive preachers of children's sermons can accomplish this combination, and thereby retain the integrity of the cognitive and affective dimensions of faith.

The final "educational objections" (namely that children's sermons tend to be moralistic, humanistic, or legalistic) all relate to the assumptions the preachers who deliver these sermons make about the faith in general. The pastor who presents children with little lessons on "rules to live by" or "ways to succeed in life or with God" is likely to preach the same sorts of sermons to adults as well. I am not certain how such an orientation can be avoided in the training of the one who holds forth in the pulpit or with the children.

Inclusive children's sermons are ones that reflect the loving nature of God's self-revelation in the person of Jesus Christ rather than the legalistic concept that assumes one must earn God's favor by being a "good boy or girl" who is always neat, quiet, respectful, courteous, and reverent. No wonder children rebel against church when their independence begins developing in the adolescent years! Rules **destroy** individuality and support the corporate ideal of behavior and belief, while grace says that God accepts people as they are! The objections raised by the critics of children's sermons may more appropriately be leveled at an inadequate theology. Good children's sermons, like any good sermon, can avoid the moralistic/humanistic/legalistic trap.

The Theological Objection

Three of the objections raised from a theological perspective (that children's sermons make children, rather than God, the center of the message; that they assume the word in Scripture and sermon are beyond the level of children's understanding; and that many manipulate biblical texts to fit the preacher's goals), relate either directly or indirectly to the role of Scripture in the worship of the congregation and in relation to children. Once again, the poor children's sermon is convicted by these criticisms. Inclusive children's sermons, however, are inclusive of more than persons. They strive to be inclusive of the text, by directing the life-transforming power of the gospel toward the audience.

The problem with many children's sermons is their lack of emphasis on the revelatory character of both Scripture and worship. The collective witness to the centrality of Scripture in the effective worship service is overwhelming. An effective, inclusive children's sermon must be one that takes the text as seriously as it does the child who is to be presented the word contained in that text. Such an intentional orientation to the text should prohibit the preacher from humanizing the gospel in the life of the child, from withholding the Bible from the child until his or her maturity in the faith, or from manipulating the text in any way.

Willimon's objection that many children's sermons do not seem to relate to the rest of worship reflects the same problem. The children's sermon, if it is truly inclusive in nature, should be an integral part of the entire flow of the worship experience. Richard Coleman states:

> The children's sermon should not be isolated and obtrusive. Every service of corporate worship should be planned around a central theme, and the children's homily should represent a development of that theme for a particular age level. When the children's sermon is not a part of a general theme, even the most well thought-out message only reinforces the assumption that it is a nice sidelight that is occasionally included. . . . In short, the Scripture text that is the basis for the adult sermon should also be the foundation of the children's sermon—for practical as well as theological reasons.[77]

My own model for the children's sermon reflects this same belief. The inclusive children's sermon is one that upholds the integrity of Scripture and worship, rather than an intrusion into the order of things solely for the purpose of being trendy or cute.

Foster's criticism that children's sermons often place the preacher in a paternalistic role in relation to the children is based on the attitude and setting within which children's sermons are generally presented. If children perceive the preacher to be distant, aloof, and unapproachable in their general relationship to him or her, and have that perception reinforced by sitting on a pew in the front of the sanctuary with the preacher looming over them, a well-meaning sermon on God's acceptance and love will have hardly been communicated effectively. In order for children's sermons to be inclusive, they must be based upon some continuity of relationship between the preacher and the children. Any effective communicator with children must enjoy being with children; an effective preacher of children's sermons must be able to relate to the children as fellow pilgrims in the process of faith development.[78] The communication of such a desire to be inclusive may be reinforced by sharing the sermon as a friend among friends, by gathering together in a circle, all sitting on the floor, or by other creative setting alterations.

The community of faith, the body of Christ within which the children come to experience the love and grace of God in present reality and personal relationships, must be guided toward a healthy relationship with the one who delivers the children's sermons. The powerful authority that children and many adults give to the minister must be intentionally dealt with by the preacher, so that the way in which he or she relates with the children will show acceptance, love, and sincerity instead of paternalism.

The Inclusion/Exclusion Objection

The most valid of the criticisms raised to children's sermons are the ones that deal with the authors' impressions that these sermons in some way promote the exclusion of children from the full life of participation in the body of Christ, rather than their inclusion in that same body. There is certainly a danger that the attention to the needs of one group to the exclusion (intentional or not) of others negates the God-given inclusiveness of the community at worship.

However, I believe the children's sermon to be a statement directed to the children and to the congregation simultaneously that, in *this* congregation, children are considered important, that we accept them, and that we wish to relate the gospel directly to them in a special way. The controlling theme of a worship service is carried in more than one form. Worship is not only preaching, nor is it merely the celebration of the Eucharist/Lord's Supper/communion. The text is heard, responded to, sung, prayed, acted out, read, and shared. It takes several different forms, is expressed in several different images, and is experienced in several different ways in each service of worship. I fail to see how the presentation of the theme gathered from the text that gives worship its integrity, in a setting with children and in images appropriate to their experiences and understanding, detracts from the inclusive nature of worship with the body of Christ. Children's sermons that are sensitive to the integrity of children, the integrity of the community, and the integrity of the text within the context of worship, are by their very nature inclusive of children within the body of Christ. When children are fully a part of worship, a separate sermon does not exclude!

59

Inclusive Children's Sermons: Some Assumptions

Several assumptions about children's sermons guide the organization of this section:

Children's sermons are a legitimate means of communicating the gospel within the context of worship. They can communicate to children the inclusive nature of the body of Christ by demonstrating Christian love and acceptance of their importance in action, rather than in words.

They also communicate the gospel to the others in worship. First, the other people who participate in worship participate in the children's sermon in the same way children participate in the rest of the worship experience. Fred Craddock speaks of the process of "overhearing the gospel," by which he means the manner in which worshipers frequently tune in and out at various points in the worship service.[79] Because of this episodic character of the worshiper (which developmentalists have demonstrated to be characteristic of children as well), Craddock maintains that the message one receives from a worship experience is one received from a safe distance, one that is "overheard" as it communicates with "someone else." The parables of Jesus utilize this technique effectively, as the Pharisees, teachers, disciples, and others are brought into the story as interested observers, only to be told, with King David in 2 Samuel 12, "**You** are the one!" Children do not worship in isolation when they are in the children's sermon; the others are "overhearing the gospel," and are possibly receiving a word of grace from it as well. The children's sermon can remind the adults worshiping with the children of the contributions childlikeness and childhood can make to the fully lived life of faith.

The children's sermon should be tied to the scriptural references that give a central focus to the worship service. The congregation I presently serve uses the lectionary that the Disciples share with other denominations. In each service, we make a conscious attempt to have all of the prayers, responses, hymns, anthem, calls to participation, and other acts of worship reflect the theme presented early in the service by the reading of the Scripture. The children's sermon should reflect the same theme as the rest of the service, as a further means of reinforcing the message the word proclaims that day.

The children's sermon should utilize images, symbols, and categories that communicate well with children. This, in turn, involves two further assumptions: first, that the person who would preach a children's sermon should know her or his audience. Each gathering of children is somewhat different from the previous one; the group might be primarily children from the fifth and sixth grades one week and entirely preschoolers the next. Agricultural images, which would work well with the rural nature of one part of the country, might not speak well at all to a child from Bedford-Stuyvesant. An awareness of the events occurring in the life of the community and the lives of the children themselves will greatly affect the selection of an appropriate image to communicate the essence of the good news in a given setting. Secondly, the images selected should respect the developmental differences of children at different stages of both cognitive and faith development. While sin is a legitimate theological concept that a Christian needs eventually to understand, an attempt to explain sin as a category will not be as effective with children as allowing them first to experience sin through drama, role-playing, or story-telling and then identifying the term. An awareness of the characteristics of children at various ages helps one to speak appropriately with children.

Children's sermons should be informal, participative, challenging, and simple. They should involve movement and invite the children to draw their own conclusions. Andrew Weaver suggests six rules for the preacher of children's sermons: (1) think playfully, (2) think drama, (3) think present, (4) think participation, (5) think real, and (6) think simple.[80]

The preacher of children's sermons should know her or his own faith. One who does not know what he or she believes will be restricted in the ability to communicate anything of meaning to others, and children have the uncanny knack of spotting a fake a mile away.

The image or images chosen should point to and open up the message, not distract the child's attention from it. This is one of the dangers of the object lesson approach to children's sermons, although not a danger exclusive to this one form.

Finally, the invitation to the children's sermon should be an open invitation. The majority of children who participate in children's sermons will be between the ages of four and ten (the latter part of Stage 1 and all of Stage 2 on the chart in Chapter Two), but the invitation to this portion of worship should allow the children in attendance to decide for themselves whether or not to participate.

Thus, the objections generally raised against the inclusion of children's sermons in worship are invalidated when the children's sermons being presented are truly inclusive of the children within the body of Christ, of the message revealed in the Scripture that governs the shared experience of worship, and of the integrity of the service of worship itself. When the children's sermon is sensitively and carefully prepared, it can be a powerful instrument by which the children of the congregation can come to see themselves as an integral part of the body of Christ. Children's sermons that are intentionally inclusive reveal the grace to be found within the body of Christ.

Chapter Five

Inclusive Children's Sermons: A Model for Proceeding

The inclusive children's sermon is one that begins to take the children's sermon seriously as a legitimate form of communication of the gospel. The inclusive children's sermon is a **sermon,** and must be given the same thoughtful preparation and attention to detail, style, text, and audience as any good sermon. The purpose of this fifth chapter is to present a model for inclusive children's sermons. The person preparing the children's sermon should consider the following six steps: attitude, setting, audience, content, form, and images.

The Model

Attitude

Before the hymn begins, before the Scripture is read, even before the organist (or pianist) begins the prelude, the first event of worship has occurred. It occurs when the worshipers enter the sanctuary and encounter each other in the context of a gathered community coming together to praise God and to share in the fellowship that is possible with the empowerment of God. Before we begin the act of worshiping God we have impressions of God, of the body of Christ, and of ourselves in relation to both. Children are especially involved in this process of interpreting their feelings about worship, because the emotive component of life is dominant over the cognitive, rational side. The attitude one brings to an experience of worship is crucial to the experience one will have in worship.

Before the children's sermon begins one needs to consider the issue of attitude, which comes into play on three fronts. The first of these is the **attitude of the congregation.** I have suggested in the first chapter that the attitude of the congregation toward the worshiping child is vital in the communication of the biblical message of the inclusion of all persons, regardless of age, sex, color, or any other artificial distinction. An uncaring, cold, indifferent, or antagonistic congregation cannot communicate to children the sense of acceptance, of relatedness to the body of Christ, of the importance adults attach to their faith, or of the corporate nature of the church. It cannot show the life-affirming, celebrative nature of the biblical witness, the variety of expression of God's word, their connectedness with the "old, old story," what is expected of children as the church, or the more mature view of faith awaiting them in their later development.

Only an open, caring, sharing, responsive congregation can communicate all the advantages suggested in Chapter Three that children may gain from participation with adults in worship. Before children's sermons can become an effective means of communicating the love of God to a seven-year-old boy who has recently lost his father, the congregation must be willing to minister to that child's needs. It does little good to proclaim, "God loves you," when it is painfully obvious that no one in the congregation, the only visible body the child can see for the Christ we proclaim, regards him with respect or acceptance, while all ignore his grief. Congregational attitude toward the children's sermon is but a portion of its attitude toward children in general, and children in worship in particular. Therefore, the first agenda in developing inclusive children's sermons would seem to be the development of an inclusive congregation.

Such a task is awesome in scope, while simple in intent. All of us who serve the church in one capacity or another express the desire for this to begin in our congregations or other communities of faith. Yet no clear direction seems to have emerged to accomplish this desired result. One principle seems to be consistently applicable: one learns best by doing. The congregation that wishes to be more inclusive needs to consciously decide to begin including those it has systematically excluded in the past. This would seem to be an effective way to begin altering a negative congregational attitude toward children in worship, and specifically toward the children's sermon.

The second attitudinal front is that of the minister, pastor, or preacher who will be in sermon with the children. Before this person can effectively communicate the message he or she is commissioned to proclaim, the children whom she or he will address and with whom he or she will converse must develop a trusting relationship with that person. Like any relationship, like the appreciation of worship in general, the development of trust in relation to the preacher of the children's sermon is a cumulative effect engendered in experiencing her as trustworthy in a variety of settings, and seeing him as a warm, open, communicative person over a period of time. Barring direct revelation, a person does not come to faith from one experience of worship in isolation. Barring such a thing as "love at first sight," a child does not come to trust and respect the preacher on first impression either.

The one who would deliver children's sermons must cultivate his or her relationship with the children who would be the audience for the sermons in a variety of settings associated with the church: in the family home, in the church hallways, in church school classes, when chancing to meet them in local stores, and as they ride past the church building on their bicycles. The only way children's sermons will be consistently isolating experiences for children is if they are the only positive relationship ever developed with the preacher of those sermons. Conversely, the preacher of children's sermons who would wish to make them inclusive of children must develop a positive, affirmative attitude toward and with the children with whom they will be shared.

The one who would deliver children's sermons must also become like a child himself or herself. It is just as difficult to relate well with children without, in essence, becoming a child oneself as it is to understand a parable without first entering into the world of parabolic thinking. Jerome Berryman's article, "Being in Parables with Children"[81] and Sallie McFague's book *Speaking in Parables*[82] both address the power of parables as metaphor in engaging the reader in sharing the life-world of the parable itself. Parables "convict" us because of their ability to draw us into them "as children," as participants (even from afar), and as fellow travelers along the rocky path, the thorny trail, and the good soil, joining the farmer in spreading the seed.

Likewise, communication with children must begin with an ability to become childlike ourselves. While a person may certainly learn how to speak to children, it is only the person who can become a child for a few moments, who can truly play, and can let go of the sophisticated, proper, mature demeanor of the "parent" (to borrow a term used by transactional analysis), even for a while, who can really communicate with children.

The preacher of the children's sermon must develop his or her own childlikeness in order to provide a suitably comfortable and communi-

65

cative attitude toward children. She or he must enter into the parables, metaphors, images, and symbols of the faith with the children in order to communicate them to children.

The final attitudinal front is that of the children themselves. Children are naturally spontaneous, energetic, and awed by the mysteries of life. They feel a need to be affirmed as persons, and can in return give the most affirmative "strokes" imaginable. The imagination by which the children of preschool and the early school years make sense of their world and join together the separate episodes of life can be a potent ally in the appropriation of faith by children. We need to be aware of the attitudes that children bring with them to worship, to praise those that are positive, and to accept children as persons even when their attitudes are less than admirable.

Setting

The issue of setting for the children's sermon must be addressed on two levels: liturgical setting and physical setting.

Liturgical Setting. Every order of worship has some order to it; that is why it is called an **order** of worship! Distinctive orders of worship in a given religious tradition or a particular congregation develop in the direction they do because the form has something to communicate that the people who worship wish to convey or to celebrate. Thus the placement of the children's sermon within the order of worship should be carefully considered. Because it will have most of its content determined by the scriptural texts, it should necessarily follow the careful, expressive reading of that selection from the Bible, although not necessarily following it immediately.

Since the children's sermon is "proclamation," it would be appropriate to place it in a spot in the order of worship where proclamation has been prepared by text, prayer, and song. In our congregation the children's sermon is placed near the beginning of the service, following the opening section, identified as "Praise to God" (which includes the call to worship, a hymn of praise, the invocation and congregational repetition of the Lord's Prayer, and the "Gloria Patri"), and at the end of the second section, marked "Fellowship and Prayer" (which includes the concerns of the church, Scripture readings, a hymn of prayer, silent prayer, and the pastoral prayer).

It is also important to point out the event of worship that immediately follows the children's sermon in our order of worship: the celebration of communion, or the Lord's Supper. Liturgical historians tell us that the early church brought catechumens into the service of

66

worship through the "Service of the Word," through the reading and interpretation of the Scripture, before dismissing them to further instruction as the confirmed members of the church gathered together around the Eucharist.[83]

The real reason for locating the children's sermon where it now resides had more pragmatic reasoning behind it. In its present location, the child who participates in the children's sermon has the benefit of being introduced to the congregation's singing of the words of faith, hearing and responding to the Scripture, public and private prayer, the recitation of the events important to the life of the congregation and a call to personal participation in worship, while still having the children's sermon early enough in the service that very young or very restless children may exit quietly and contentedly once "their time" is over. What we have found is what we had hoped to find: once the children see that there is a time for them where they will be related to on their own level and in their own terms, they have little trouble remaining through the rest of the service. Their presence in worship begins to make more and more sense to them and to the rest of the congregation.

Physical Setting. The other level of this section concerns the physical setting for the children's sermon. The foremost consideration in this regard concerns proximity to the center of focus for most of worship, that is, in or near the chancel of the sanctuary. It is from this place that the word of God is made known through Scripture and the breaking of bread. While my own tradition has consistently "desacralized" the place of worship (we have "communion tables" instead of "altars," for instance), there is still something powerfully symbolic about the place from which the word is proclaimed and blessed for one's personal partaking. The children probably sense the symbolic power of the sanctuary much more strongly than do the adults who worship with them. Therefore, the location of the children's sermon near the supposed source of that mystery we call faith provides the proper setting for the children's sermon.

In a recent article by James Carr, the very act of the children's movement to their "place" is singled out as contributing to their means of relating to the experience of worship. Carr states that such an act of movement involves the sensorimotor response of children to worship, and that such an active, whole-body, sensory experience can assist in developing a sense of ownership in both the place and the experience of worship there.[84]

Carr also argues that the fully sensory engagement of children in worship is to be desired. In his understanding, the oral-aural (speaking-

67

hearing) experience gives more structure to the "space" of worship than does any other sense. In distinguishing it from the visual experience (which he argues elsewhere to be an important element in the worship experience), Carr states:

> The essential difference in the aural and visual experiences . . . is that persons stand in front of visual fields which they apprehend and dissect in a "succession of 'fixes' " whereas acoustic fields give persons a sense of immediacy, involvement, and process which must be experienced in its wholeness in a single movement.[85]

It is, indeed, the verbal character of the children's sermon that helps to convey the attitude, as well as the message, of the gospel and its representatives to children.

I am acutely aware of the powerful bearing I carry physically in relation to the children in worship. Being six feet tall, of medium build, thickly bearded with black hair, and clad in robes, I could easily overwhelm a child by standing over him or her as he or she sat in the pew. I therefore call the children to gather around me at the entrance to the Chancel, and we all sit together on the floor. Thus, the powerful, potentially intimidating presence I might convey to the child is dissipated as we sit together as equals. I try to have each child within an arm's reach, if at all possible. Thus, the potential of communication by touch, as well as by words, is ever present. The "acoustic field" becomes joined with a tactile field by such an action.

It is also helpful to make provision for plenty of room for movement, if the direction of the children's sermon should require it. Children, particularly those of a younger age, appreciate movement, which gives them a sense of self-expression that their still-developing vocabularies often prohibit. Making certain that there is sufficient space for any eventuality in the form of the children's sermon gives a sense of continuity to the experience: this is their time, and this is also their space. Such a sense of dependable ownership of the worship service reinforces the content of the sermon itself, and the entire worship experience is enhanced.

Audience

The specific age-range, composition, orientation, and past experiences in the body of Christ of the children participating in the children's sermon will vary from congregation to congregation, and frequently from week to week! Therefore a major part of the earlier suggestions regarding the attitude of the preacher toward the children would be the admonition, "Know thy audience!"

It is important for the preacher, whether of children's sermons or of any other kind of sermon, to know the basic character of the individuals with whom he or she would be sharing the good news. The insights of developmental psychology and faith development studies might suggest a uniformity and unalterable nature to the development of certain logical and moral characteristics in the personality; they are termed universal, hierarchical, linear, and consistent. However, it is important to note that, for Erikson at least, the "epigenetic" principle is only claimed to be consistent in its **order** of ascendancy, not in its **time** of ascendancy.[86] In discussing Fowler's work, Donald Miller sees him taking Erikson's caveat a step further: "Unlike Erikson, Fowler does not insist that persons inevitably move from one stage to another. A person may live his or her life in a stage-three faith."[87]

There are therefore at least five things the preacher of children's sermons should know about her or his audience: the character of the community in which they live, the extent of the training the children have received in their academic settings (as well as their church setting), the age group of the children who will be likely to participate in the children's sermons, the developmental levels of the individuals to be involved, and the special problems operative within the group.

Knowledge of the character of the community within which most of the children live will be helpful for two primary reasons: it will help the preacher of the children's sermon determine what the community holds as central to the meaning of life and the living of faith, and it will help him or her avoid the use of examples, objects, and images that are not appropriable by the children in the sermon with him or her. The former point is another part of the process of coming to know the children with whom one will be working, while the latter is merely a part of the process of good, effective communication. It would be useless, for instance, to develop a sermon around the process of shrimping, which is done by dragging a net behind the boat, and then separating the crabs, stingray, and flounder from the shrimp, no matter how well it might communicate the story of the sheep and the goats, if the audience is located on the plains of western Kansas. The form and images by which the content of the sermon is to be communicated must have integrity, a connectedness with the community as well as with the text, the order of worship, and the lives of the children.

It is also evident that individual congregations, like individual people, vary in their faith development. The congregation that is intentional about its education and pastoral nurture of its members and does a good job of providing a setting that encourages and enables constructive learning will most likely send children to the worship service better prepared to receive and to process a word of grace than would a congregation that provides only the barest minimum of educational opportunities and little nurture. Worship should never exist as an entity separate from the educational enterprise of the congregation, lest either of these begin to suffer from delusions of grandeur. Knowing how well the congregation trains its members in the living out of the faith to which they are heir can help the preacher of children's sermons know what the corporate myths, shared language, and common beliefs of the community are. This would allow her or him to communicate more effectively in terms the children could appropriate.

The normal age-groups for children's sermons would seem to be those children between the ages of late in the fourth year and early in the tenth.[88] My experience with children's sermons has born out what others have said, that the children below Erikson's second level of early childhood (ages four to five, characterized by the crisis of "Initiative vs. Guilt") will probably not find the children's sermon very rewarding, and will find the nursery and its activities more interesting, while the child of the preadolescent years (eleven to twelve) will begin to feel uncomfortable with the littler children and contend that the sermons are "babyish." I notice, however, that those who have by conscious decision moved out of the "circle" of the children's sermon still listen very intently to what is said, a characteristic very common in children of that age who struggle with their childhood identities and their growing bodies.

The audience for most children's sermons, then, will be composed primarily of children from the second part of Stage 1 (age four and five) through the end of Stage 2 (approximately age ten to twelve). It is important to remember, however, that each congregation develops its own personality, so that the age-group of such a gathering in one particular congregation might be significantly higher or lower than the normal. My own practice, when coming to the time in the service for the children's sermon, is to simply say, "Will our children come forward, please?" and then leave the decision-making responsibility with the individual child. This respects the individuality of the children involved.

In addition to respecting the decisions of the individuals we must also respect the differences that exist between the participants of a children's sermon in terms of their developmental levels or individual stages of faith development. There are at least seven contributions the related fields of cognitive and faith development studies make to our understanding of the children with whom we worship and with whom we share children's sermons: (1) a recognition of, respect for, and deter-

70

mination to deal with the **individuality** of each person at his or her own level of development; (2) an understanding of the **rational processes** of children, which might help us find ways of communicating appropriately with children "where they are"; (3) a sensitization to the **value-free nature** of development; (4) attention to the **social nature of learning,** which calls adults to greater participation with children in their learning processes; (5) help in **restructuring of one's world** through the taking of a new perspective by resolving one's stage crisis; (6) understanding and relating to **components of one level higher** than one's own development, so that the presentation of arguments from such a higher level might draw him or her toward that growth we all desire for our children; and (7) recognition of the importance of the **order of ascendancy** of life issues, rather than their specific time of ascendancy.

In her article entitled, "The Original Vision: Children and Religious Experience," Maria Harris asks a pertinent question for our discussion of children's sermons: "How (do we) marry the images in the tradition with the images experienced by the young person without doing damage to either?"[89] She answers her own question a page later, arguing that such images need to be "appropriate to" and "appropriable by" the child, while constantly being aware that these images are, at best, approximations of the reality to which they point.[90]

It is the two-edged issue of "appropriate to" and "appropriable by" that is addressed by faith development and the other developmental approaches. The children who are the audience of children's sermons come from the later part of one stage (Stage 1) and the early to middle part of the next (Stage 2). Therefore, knowing the developmental characteristics of children in these two stages might help us be "appropriate to" these children, and to present images that are "appropriable by" them.

Nothing that is not appropriable by a child can be considered appropriate to him or her. The considerable work of Fowler, Erikson, Piaget, and many others might help us understand our audience more fully, so that we might communicate the experience of faith more appropriately with children.

Content

The content of the inclusive children's sermon is the revelation of God's grace in the person of Jesus Christ. Sallie McFague says that the story of Jesus is the story *par excellence* for Christians.[91] It is necessary, then, for the relating of that story, which provides the essential content of faith, to be based around the Scripture that has told us that "old, old story" for centuries.

The starting point for the content of inclusive children's sermons is Scripture.[92] While this should seem self-evident, most children's sermons in congregations around the country would belie that. Many children's sermons are experienced as shallow and trite because they have not first been grounded in a thorough exegetical examination of the biblical text. The Scripture centers us as worshipers in the continuing self-revelation of God.

Thus, the first "act" of developing an inclusive children's sermon is an engagement of the texts of worship. I have adopted, in the last several years, the use of the Disciples/Presbyterian/UCC form of the COCU lectionary, and have done so for a number of reasons. The chief of these is the intent of the lectionary to carry on a consistent, progressive journey through the Bible. The lectionary gives a thematic unity to worship as a cumulative experience that is lost in the rather haphazard way in which many preachers choose texts for sermons (which is to sit down, thumb through the Bible, and wait for a text to present itself!). By using the lectionary, I begin to feel a sense of connectedness with my theological tradition.

The children's sermon is like any other sermon: it ought to begin with the text, because the act of proclamation is not an isolated event but rather the proclamation of the word revealed through Scripture. The children's sermon ought to deal with the same text that gives rise to the sermon, and should benefit from the same exegetical care that goes into the proclamation of any good sermon. Our model requires that the children's sermon reflect the same theme that is preached in the sermon and that both be derived from the process of lifting the content or message "out of" ("ex") the life-world of the lectionary readings for the day. The application of sound hermeneutical principles to that message is then possible.[93] The rationale for this requirement is simple: the given lectionary texts provide the thematic unity for the entire experience of worship, of which the children's sermon is an integral part.

Thus, there are some givens as one begins the process of developing children's sermons. The first is attitudinal, on the part of the congregation, the preacher, and the children involved; the second is the setting, both liturgical and physical; the third is the texts of worship, presented by the lectionary and the church seasons. It is only as I accept and integrate these givens into my own experience and understanding of faith that I may approach the text that will provide the foundation for inclusive children's sermons as a person prepared for appropriate exegesis.

72

I am convinced that every passage of Scripture has something to say to the people of God whom we call the body of Christ. This is not to claim that all passages are equally powerful or have something correct, positive, or constructive to say; it is only to state the belief that each passage can be proclaimed, if one works at the exegesis diligently enough. What one does in exegeting a passage is to fold back the layers of tradition, lay bare the message often obscured by language we no longer understand, and thereby release the word of grace that lies behind a text. It is this word of grace that begs to be proclaimed, but we often preach or teach one of the layers that cover it up. Therefore, the first step in developing the inclusive children's sermon is the attempt, through the exegesis of the texts of worship, which also produce the sermon and the thematic structure for the whole of worship, to get at the core of the message being revealed in the Scripture for that occasion.

An inclusive children's sermon is one that respects the integrity of the texts of worship. Such a sermon would be likely to avoid the pitfall of centering on the children rather than on the texts' revelation of the God of grace. Responsible preaching of any kind must relate to the biblical witness on its own terms rather than bring the preacher's agenda to the text. The same must be true for the inclusive children's sermon. It must deal with the central message conveyed by the texts being presented on a given Sunday.

This, however, can often present a problem when relating lectionary texts to children. Children are best served when there are few major points being made in a sermon or lesson. The episodic nature of the thought processes in the earlier stages of those children who participate in children's sermons almost demands that the children's sermon make a single point. Even the more narrative thought of the later-staged children would incorporate a single point, housed in an engaging story or drama, more readily than several important but often competing points. In his book on children's sermons, Richard Coleman relates a crucial point made by one of his mentors, Paul Scherer: "(he) also emphasized the value of being sure that each sermon has one central point, and that everything flows toward and away from that point."[94] While this is wise counsel for any sermon, it is especially appropriate in relation to the children's sermon.

The problem comes in the fact that the lectionary presents us with three texts, not one, which do not always present a unified theme around which to base the sermon. The preacher of the children's sermon is frequently faced with the decision of how much of the text or texts to include in the sermon. It is a dilemma that also affects the preparation of the adult sermon. As I approach the lections for the day, after the

73

exegetical investigation of them, I ask: What in these texts speaks more clearly and most revealingly to the needs and concerns of this congregation, and to the prophetic nature of the word? The process by which one begins to bring the word of God to bear upon the worshipers must include all of those features that normally precede the exposition of scripture. This hermeneutical task involves a number of frames of reference. Jack Seymour and Carol Wehrheim state, "Therefore, since the interpreter comes to an experience or text with a frame of reference, the task is to seek to understand how that frame of reference may illumine or block the meaning that is created."[95] The preacher of children's sermons is an interpreter of revealed meaning, and at least a portion of her or his task must be to run the texts through the "filters" of his or her own experience. Thus, the question addressed to the lectionary texts becomes at least partially a question of personal engagement in interpretation, an engagement that should, ultimately, lead to the illumination, the making appropriate, of the texts in the lives of the people.

This process needs to result in the choice of a single theme that is theologically and exegetically accurate. As a means of reinforcing the centrality of the theme chosen, which has emerged from this hermeneutical process, our congregation makes that theme the controlling theme for the many elements of the worship experience. It is not enough for the children's sermon to "mirror" the sermon and the Scripture readings. These are but a part (although a crucial part) of the overall experience that is worship. If a theme emerges from the exegetical and hermeneutical tasks as the focus of the word, that theme needs also to be at the center of the rest of the service. The one way to ensure that the children's sermon is not an isolated, obtrusive incident in worship is for it to become a partner in a thoroughgoing structuring of the worship experience around a central, biblically based theme that utilizes all of the forms available in worship to communicate its message—the word of grace.

The content of inclusive children's sermons, then, is dependent upon sound exegesis of the given lectionary texts, the application of a sensitive hermeneutical engagement of the texts, the focus of the findings of these two tasks to a single unifying theme, and the application of that theme to the entire experience of worship.

A caveat is in order in this discussion of content. There is a tendency among adults to equate content with reality. We have a built-in impression (or prejudice, if you will) that says that an accurate, consistent, intellectually integrated content is the goal of any process of communicating the word. Communication is rarely made solely on the basis of such cognitive, intellectual terms. We have much more nonverbal, affective communication than verbal and intellectual. This is especially true in relation to children. The caveat that needs to be raised is that, with children, the application of these sound exegetical, hermeneutical, and liturgical processes cannot stop at the development of a set of propositions to be presented. That does not constitute content for children as much as affect, feeling, and the imaginative structure of reality. Whenever we address the issue of content with children, we must be aware that what we say is only a portion of what we communicate. Thus the process of developing the content of a children's sermon must also deal with attitude once again. This caveat works in both a positive and a negative direction. Coleman states:

> Tone is important whenever we communicate, but it is even more important when we communicate with children. The content of a message may prove to be irrelevant, untimely, or aimed at an age level different from the group we are addressing. But children almost always pick up the tone of the message. Various studies have demonstrated that children are particularly influenced by their assessment of the speaker's intentions and the meaning of the situation. Since younger children are less confident about the use of language, they give more weight to nonlinguistic clues, which they understand better. This factor can work both to our advantage and our disadvantage. On the one hand, we need not despair if children miss the central point of a message; the tone of a sermon may succeed when the content fails.[96]

The negative component of the caveat is the temptation to so focus on the "tone" or attitude that the meaning behind it is lost in the cloud of "relevance" and "feeling." The content of the inclusive children's sermon must, as Coleman also claims, mesh with its tone.

Form

The content of a biblical text or texts does not suddenly appear to the reader in a pure, usable revelation; it is given to us through particular forms. "The form in which a particular message is cast is also important in a still stricter sense of the word 'form,' for a 'form' is never just something external, concerned with literary style alone; in the last resort, form cannot be separated from content."[97] The words are those of Gerhard von Rad, one of the most influential of this century's Old Testament scholars. While not the founder of the form-critical school of biblical studies, Von Rad may certainly be regarded as one of its greatest practitioners. This quotation seems an appropriate way to begin an investigation of the form or forms to be utilized in inclusive children's sermons. The basic thesis regarding the relationship between content and form is that form follows function or, in this case, content. Yet, it must be admitted that there is always an inseparable connection between the two.

In his discussion of the parables, Jerome Berryman treats John D. Crossan's understanding of that biblical form, and concludes that Crossan saw parables as a metaphor extended to a narrative, then states that a parable is "a use of language which requires participation in the metaphor to evoke the referrent."[98] I would extend his argument to include **all** of the forms by which the gospel may be communicated. A form always requires the reader or hearer to enter into its world before it may completely open up the message it contains.

Much care should be given to the selection of the form by which the content of a children's sermon is conveyed. There are any number of available forms from which the preacher may choose: sermon, song, story, drama, object lessons, movement, dance, etc. The specific form chosen for a children's sermon must always fit the content that the preceding steps have revealed.

The best way of proceeding at this stage of the process is to ask the question: What is the best form available to help make this point? The attempt should always be made to choose a form that reflects the tone of the passage one is interpreting. There is no single form that will always be applicable to a given text. Therefore, the character of this step might be described as a "survey of forms."

What the preacher is looking for in the uniting of content and form is a form that allows the text to do the same work it did in its biblical setting. Thus, the preacher must constantly be aware of both the preceding steps in the development of the sermon and the nature and impact of the text itself. Since the preacher of children's sermons is dealing with an audience with a more limited range of cognitive abilities and affective sympathies, he or she has a narrow range of possible forms. The most common forms chosen for children's sermons are "object lessons," drama (participatory story), and story.

Object Lesson Form. The object lesson form is the utilization of an object, or prop, that is held before the children, and followed by a question of recognition, such as, "What is this?" Once the children respond, the preacher proceeds to make some point of analogy between the object and the situation of children, the message of the text, or some other means of identification between it and the point of the sermon. The object lesson has the advantage that it is able to combine the oral-aural sense with the visual sense, thus engaging the children involved in the sermon in more than one sensory experience (something appreciated by children). It is possible (indeed, probable) that, as Jesus told the parable of the sower, he had some seed in his hand, which he sowed as he spoke. This visual stimulation might reinforce the point that words alone might fail in making.

There are a multitude of object lesson books available in local bookstores. But all of them have risks as well as values. The major problem with the object lesson form is that the reliance on an external object runs the risk of distracting the attention of the children from the point the preacher is trying to make. The reason this is such a present danger is that children are basically episodic during much of the age-range covered by the children's sermon, and giving them something on which they can focus their attention, and then asking them to move from that to another focus (the preacher's analogy) risks leaving the audience back at the object.

A further drawback of the object lesson form is that it, more than any other form, tends to become "cute." This happens for obvious reasons; the object itself is frequently something designed to catch the attention through its incongruity with the rest of the surroundings in the worship service. The reaction to such a design is delight, enchantment, or amazement, but the base reaction (by the congregation at least) seems to be, "Isn't that clever/cute/sweet!" While object lessons might do an excellent job of drawing together disparate sensory experiences, they should be employed with caution, and with a definite purpose in mind. The hurried or harried preacher of children's sermons can often fall victim to the temptation to employ a "prop" as a "crutch," rescuing her or him from the thorough process of preparation demanded by any sermon. One rule of thumb that should apply to the object lesson form of children's sermons is that a sermon that draws attention to an object needs at least twice the normal preparatory attention to the subject. This could become a considerable amount of time in light of the standard recommendations regarding the ratio of time spent in preparation as compared to time in the sermon!

This is not to totally discount the efficacy of the object lesson form of the children's sermon. A well-planned, structured, creative use of visual aid, object, puppet, or other "prop" that deals with the thematic structure of worship and respects the integrity of the children may prove to be the best choice of form for preaching the sermon. The point is simply that, in light of the inherent dangers of misdirection of the children's attention and the tendency to "get cute" with an object, the use of this form may require more discipline on the part of the preacher in the process of preparation. The sermon entitled "Shouting Stones," in Chapter Six is an example of an "inclusive" children's sermon using the object lesson form.

77

Drama or Participatory Story Form. The second major category of children's sermons is the use of the drama or participatory story form. The primary thrust of this form is the intent of the sermon to involve the children in the action of the story, through such techniques as role-playing, encouraging the children to provide the sound effects for the story, mime, or having a story "acted out" by persons from the audience. In this form the children are encouraged to enter the action of the story through taking the perspective of another person. Its major positive feature is that drama and personal participation appeal to the heightened sense of imagination and fantasy that at least partially describe the thought processes of the children most likely touched by a children's sermon. And, because it **is** drama, such a form may communicate deep truths that prose, narrative, sermon, lecture, and exhortation do not. Drama has the ability to transcend the drabness of everyday communication while still presenting both everyday situations and everyday language, housed perhaps in a form that pulls more strongly at the poetic (possibly even childlike) side of a person's existence.

The primary drawback of this form is the very essence of one's participation in the action and impact of drama: the process of perspective taking. Developmentalists have demonstrated that children in Stage 1 have a difficult time taking the perspective of another person, due both to the inability to either generalize from their own experience to that of another person and to the inherent egocentrism of this stage. And, while perspective taking is one of the agenda issues of the Stage 2 child, this process is still latent during most of the years covering the audience for children's sermons. What perspective taking or empathy children of Stage 2 develop is essentially of a rudimentary nature and quite concrete. One of the major factors making drama so effective in releasing the creative side of persons, the ability to see oneself more clearly through the analogous situation of the characters in a drama, may lose some of its power with children.

Drama or participatory story as a form needs also to be thought through carefully. It is wise to ask oneself, when developing a sermon in this form, "What do I intend to have happen in the lives of these children through their participation in this drama?" A drama that does not have the thrust of the gospel, concern for the faith of the children, and a purpose behind it will be meaningless and trivial even if it is entertaining. If the purpose of the children's sermon has deteriorated to the point that entertainment is its only value, it no longer has any connection with the word to be proclaimed and should be excised from the service of worship. The sermon entitled "The Wall" is an example of the drama or participatory story form.

Story Form. Children's sermons, if properly prepared and framed within the story form, can proclaim the good news in yet another way. Story is almost always a new way of telling the good news because story, like drama, catches the hearer up in its world. Charles Foster shares four assumptions about stories that are helpful here: (a) "Stories help us and our children make sense out of our worlds"; (b) "Stories provide clues for children and ourselves regarding who we are"; (c) "Stories fill the wellsprings of our imaginations"; and (d) "Stories enable us to face up to the ambiguities of life."[99] Thus stories help children deal with three elemental aspects of being children: the issue of "world-coherence"; the issue of identity; and the issue of imagination.

The story form should be an effective way of communicating the word with children. My experience with children's sermons in this form would bear out this impression. The only real drawback with regard to this form is that it is often difficult to develop a truly good, creative story that will communicate in a new way what the biblical text has already said. There are not many good storytellers in the world these days. Most of us have been co-opted by legal forms, "Kate Turabian style," and the reporting methods of our denominational bureaucrats. It is a true challenge to tell inclusive, communicative stories these days. Perhaps the forays of Wilder, McFague, Crossan, Berryman, and others will eventuate in freeing more of us frustrated poets and storytellers from the shackles of our prosaic prisons. But, until then, the story form in children's sermons will probably be done well by very few of us.

Because both drama and story require involving children in the event itself, the same reservations expressed in relation to drama should apply to the story as well. It would be well to also begin developing a story sermon with the question, "What experience of the nature of God, or what insight into the text, do I hope this story will communicate with these children?" The story form of the children's sermon must be as much the servant of the text and of the children as any other form. An example of the story form is found in the sermon entitled "Two Rowdy Boys" in Chapter Six.

Other Forms. There are several additional forms available for us in developing children's sermons. Among these are music, dance, and art (all forms of engagement and movement, as well as imagination), prayer and the practice of the contemplative life, various forms of nonverbal communication (such as expressing emotions, feelings, and reactions to a point made in the sermon nonverbally), question-and-answer, conversation, dialogue, "let's pretend," and so forth.[100] The form of a children's sermon is limited only by the imagination and ability of the persons delivering it. There is virtually no possible form by which a sermon may be preached that would not also be applicable to a children's sermon.

The form chosen should be capable of telling the same story as that told in the text, while doing so from a fresh, engaging perspective that communicates the same spirit as that revealed by the text. Form follows content; content is communicated by form. This step in the development of inclusive children's sermons is every bit as crucial as the ones preceding it. Choose the form wisely and with great consideration.

Images

Martin Bell, an Episcopal clergyperson, wrote a marvelous book a few years ago, *The Way of the Wolf*.[101] This offering is a collection of stories, poems, and songs written by Bell, many of which are extraordinary retellings of the gospel (e.g., the first story, "Barrington Bunny," is one of the most powerful presentations of self-giving love and grace I have ever found in literature). Indeed, the subtitle of the book is indicative of the nature of Bell's work—"The Gospel in New Images."

That would also be an apt description of the inclusive children's sermons. The major difference between children and adults is not the content of their faith (which, in a Christian context, is Jesus Christ, crucified and risen), but the images by which that content is conveyed, appropriated, and internalized. Bell's images have much in common with each other: they are presented by animals, children, the downtrodden, the powerless, the unsuspected—all of which are characters and images with which children can identify their own condition. They can recognize themselves in the helplessness of a lost bunny, the search for identity of a young boy conversing with the wind, the frustrating identity-crisis of a porcupine, and so forth. In recognizing themselves and identifying with the human condition that such images present, the children are consequently opened to the power of the gospel to transform this reality.

This is the primary focus of any sermon, and especially of the inclusive children's sermon. The focus of such sermons on the development of new images by which to convey the message of the gospel to children is, therefore, appropriate. I am indebted in this portion of the model to the "hermeneutical" principles presented by Ricoeur, Wilder, McFague, and Crossan. I share with Carr an appreciation of the function of metaphoric language:

> Metaphoric thinking is primarily concerned with what persons are in the process of believing, knowing, and becoming; not with belief, knowledge,

or being as accomplished facts. . . . The primary cognitive concern here is not how to interpret metaphors in conceptual terms, but rather how the metaphor interprets life and how it can be lived.[102]

As Carr assesses the contributions of Sallie McFague to this endeavor, he lists three ways in which the perception of new images of the gospel brings about a changed consciousness of reality: (1) the path to new insights is through the recognition of "novel connections" in an otherwise familiar world (he quotes McFague, who says, "We are always children, primitives, when it comes to new insight into such matters as love, life, death, God, hope and faith."); (2) this new insight leads persons to belief through imaginative participation in images, symbols, stories—all of which fit in the concept of a metaphor; and (3) belief is worked out in life in terms of human involvement toward newly imagined possibilities. Such images keep meaning "in solution."[103]

The novel contributions of Jesus to his own religious tradition were based around his ability to make such novel connections in an otherwise familiar world. Jesus carried his audiences into a story with a set of assumptions and expectations and then, through his use of new perspectives and new images, confronted them with a shocking transformation of the world they perceived. The recognition that one has been "hooked" by the radically new perspective on reality presented by new images draws one into a personal pilgrimage toward a new way of structuring the world. And the insights of faith development literature indicate that it is just such an adoption of a new perspective that constitutes growth in cognition and faith toward the next higher stage.

Carr's following statement is a relation of McFague's insights to the children's sermon in particular.

> If children's sermons take this form of reflection and knowing seriously and seek to embody meaning in imagistic language, then they will introduce children early to a form of reflection and knowing which is thoroughly biblical . . . a good children's sermon should be an open invitation to imaginative participation in story or image or feeling, all rooted in the reality of the world. It should be an invitation to experience something familiar in a new context, even if it is, for the child, an experiencing of familiar Biblical stories in the different context of the gathered worship of the whole congregation.[104]

Inclusive children's sermons seek to do just this—to relate the good news to children in a way that will best communicate with their interests and involve them in the experience of the metaphor, story, and image operative in a biblical passage. The very "newness" of their inclusion in the worship experience of the congregation, the retelling of the gospel in images "appropriate to" and "appropriable by" children within the context of worship with all its symbolic power, will open up the content of the gospel to children in ways largely inaccessible in other settings they experience.

Engagement with the biblical texts gives us the theme for the inclusive children's sermon; the choice of a viable form by which to present this theme gives us the structure that frames the proclamation of the word with children; the development of the most powerful available images to give life to this enterprise provides access to the root meaning of the gospel story in the lives of the children involved. Where we tend to fail as "messengers" and proclaimers of the word with children, and consequently with adults as well, is by trying to interpret the metaphors, myths, and images of the faith, instead of, as Carr suggested, addressing "how the metaphor interprets life and how it can be lived."[105]

The attention to images is essentially the attention to the places in which the biblical vision of the meaningfulness of life bumps into the life-world of the children. It means addressing those things that are valued by children, such as affirmation, acceptance, affection, the value of the concrete moment, and the sense of fairness, especially as it relates to their own cases. It means entering into the life-world of children, looking through their eyes at the world around them, and choosing from their own particular field of experience those images that give a structure, a frame of reference, a fresh perspective on reality. Berryman can talk glowingly of "being in parables with children," for in our use of images we must make the moment of the children's sermon a shared experience. Thus also Jesus could speak of entering the Kingdom "as a child."

Images that seem to open up reality most effectively for children are ones with which the children can identify. Presenting such a complex story as the "Parable of the Two Debtors" in Luke 7:40–43 calls for a new image by which to convey both the nature of sin and the attitude of forgiveness manifested by Jesus. The children's sermon entitled "Two Rowdy Boys" included in Chapter Six presents mischief-makers damaging a neighbor's property and subsequently being confronted by that neighbor with the effects of their mischief. There are few children who cannot relate to either engaging in mischief or the sinking feeling in the pits of their stomachs when caught in the act and confronted with their deeds. The issue is thereby shifted from sin as a deep, dark, mysterious force in the netherworld of theological speculation to sin as a personal condition met by a forgiving and loving "neighbor" God.

The image is the life-blood of the inclusive children's sermon. It is at this stage that the preacher must take pains to immerse himself or herself in the perception of life that the children live and experience. By becoming a child oneself, one can find images "appropriate to" and "appropriable by" children.

Some Further Considerations

While the basic model I have presented calls for six steps in the preparation of the inclusive children's sermon, there are five other issues related to the sermons that need to be raised. The first has to do with length. Children have short attention spans, and the children's sermon, no matter how brilliantly conceived and creatively presented, is subject to the same time limitations as any other event in a child's life. The maximum length of the sermon should be five minutes, and this much time would only be recommended in a sermon whose form involves a drama or direct participation. A good length would be three to four minutes. The preacher need not watch her or his clock; when the sermon has run its allotted time the behavior of the children will communicate that fact more clearly than any alarm clock. The children with whom I work in my present congregation have a definite signal that says, "Time's up!" Because I wear a stole with my robe, I always have a nice gold fringe hanging within easy reach of the children. When I have lost their attention, they simply begin trying to feel or play with that fringe! Deep, heavy sighs, fidgeting bodies, rolling eyes, and picking at each other are other undeniable signals that one has lost one's audience.

The second of these considerations concerns the choice of language in the sermon. I have tried to alter my method of speaking to reflect a more inclusive language in regard to women. Thus, I make a concerted effort not to use "he" or "his" as generic terminology for all persons. The same is true in the way in which I refer to God. Rather than speaking of God as Father, I tend to use such terms as Creator or Parent. This is especially important when dealing with children, whose proclivity toward literalism can imprint a sexually limited concept of God through the appropriation of the language used by those of us with some religious authority.

The third additional consideration is the use of prayer as a means of closure for the time spent together with the children. I recommend that every children's sermon end with a prayer that pulls together the content of the sermon and thanksgiving to God for that content. This is recommended for the following reasons: prayer is the way in which many services end, thus providing an additional link between the children's sermon and the rest of worship; the prayer gives an opportunity for focusing the experience in a way that is not "preachy"; children need to be introduced to prayer as a meaningful part of worship that is tied to their own experience; and finally, it is always "right and meet" to give thanks to God for the message that the Kingdom is open to all.

The fourth consideration regards the use of organ or piano music to provide a smooth transition between the end of the children's sermon and the beginning of the next part of the service. There is movement in the sanctuary as the children return to their pews or the educational plant of the church, and a major section of the worship service is about to begin. This time takes on the character of a transitional period in worship. A brief meditation, possibly in a lighter vein than other organ and piano settings, would be an appropriate way to accomplish this transition.

The final consideration is probably the most important: by all means, **be flexible!** The natural spontaneity of children is often not kind to a preacher's sermon outline. While the asking of questions with a children's sermon is an excellent way of involving children in the event itself, the employment of this technique is not for the faint-hearted! Children do not always answer the way we hope they will, and any sermon that is not immediately adaptable in light of the serendipitous response of children is in trouble. One should prepare images that are accessible enough that different forms may be easily employed as the need arises. Working with children is always exciting, because one never knows exactly what will happen when the one uncontrollable factor in an inclusive children's sermon, the reaction and enthusiasm of the children, is applied to all one's hard work!

Inclusive Children's Sermons:
A Summary of the Model

The model here presented includes the following six steps: attitude, setting, audience, content, form, and images. The first three of these are steps that precede the direct process of developing a sermon from the texts for the particular Sunday in question. These three steps involve establishing a tone of interdependence and inclusion that will be conducive to a receptive "frame of reference" on the part of the children. The final three steps (content, form, and images) are concerned with developing an inclusive children's sermon by engagement with the biblical texts that control the thematic structure of the worship service.

The universal applicability of this model in all settings is not claimed. I have only described what has worked effectively in the two congregations I have served since completing seminary. Most congregations could, with some natural changes in light of their particular needs, make use of the model and realize some benefits in the attitudes of their children toward the church and of their adults toward both the children and their own faith. Making the church more intentionally the inclusive body of Christ through the use of inclusive children's sermons could have transforming power in the life of any congregation. I therefore submit the model to the reader with some "fear and trembling," yet confident that my experience of the benefits of such children's sermons will also be shared by others.

Chapter Six

Inclusive Children's Sermons: The Model in Practice

The purpose of this final chapter is to present some practical examples of the way in which the inclusive model for developing children's sermons is actually conducted. Three children's sermons have been selected that were delivered in lectionary Year C at the Fairhope, Alabama, Christian Church (Disciples of Christ). Each represents one of the three major forms of children's sermons identified in this discussion of the model.

The format of the three offerings is uniform: the text of the sermon is given and what actions (if any) noted. The sermon is followed by discussions of the attitude, setting, audience, content (including exegesis and the determination of theme), form, and images. An evaluation of the impact of each sermon is included.

These examples are given in the hope that they will communicate the variety of possible ways a person whose task it is to deliver children's sermons might proceed with the task. They do not intend to provide an exhaustive list of such sermons. What they intend to provide is a sense of the creativity and care that needs to be placed into the process of developing children's sermons.

Object Lesson: "Shouting Stones"

(Isaiah 59:14–20; 1 Timothy 1:12–17; Luke 19:28–40)

(As the children gather in the chancel area and take their seats on the floor close to the preacher, he or she welcomes each one informally, warmly, and sincerely. Once each child is settled in, the children's sermon begins.)

I would like to give each of you something this morning. *(Begin giving each child a small pebble or a piece of gravel as the sermon continues.)* Now, I know it's not much of a gift, but I would like you to take this small stone and look at it very closely. *(The children begin turning the stones over and over as they examine them.)* See how small and hard it is? It's solid, cold, and smooth. There's not much about this stone that makes it seem alive, is there? *(The children responded by shaking their heads back and forth, some verbalizing such things as, "No way!")* Every stone is a different size, a different shape, and a different color, like things that are alive, but none of your stones seems to be alive.

Can you imagine these stones shouting out, "Hip, hip, hooray!"? *(Several of the children giggled a bit here.)* Boy, that would be a shock, wouldn't it? *(Most of the heads nodded in the affirmative.)* Stones can't talk; they're not even alive! *(A few more giggles.)* But think with me for a few moments: How many of you have been to the park that overlooks the bay? *(The community has a municipal park on a bluff overlooking Mobile Bay; several hands were raised in response to the question, and I clarified for one child, who raised the question that this was, indeed, the park from which the Fourth of July fireworks were viewed.)* You know that great big stone monument right by the road in the park? *(Again, a few heads nodded in the affirmative.)* Well, that writing on that big stone tells about some of the people who started this town, so the people who come up to it can read some of the history of our home. **That** stone speaks, doesn't it? *(I acknowledged the nodding heads by nodding my own.)*

The stones each of you has have something special to speak about and shout about, because their job is to tell everybody that Jesus has come into our lives. Oh, your stones aren't as big as that one down in the park, and you couldn't write much on them if you tried. But the purpose of stones like that big monument downtown is to help us remember important things, and there's nothing more important than the fact that Christ has entered our lives and changed things there.

I want you to do something for me this week; will you do that? *(All the children nodded affirmatively.)* I want you to take this stone with you today, and keep it with you all week. Put it in your pocket every morning so, when you are playing, or working, or reading and happen to reach your hand into your pocket and feel this stone, it can remind you that Christ is here, and you can remember that even something as lifeless as a stone can shout out that fact. Carry this with you all week, and then bring it back with you next Sunday, when we'll talk a little more about your stones and the Jesus they shout about. Now, as you leave, after our prayer, would you help pass out these stones to the rest of the people here today? *(Bags of small pebbles had been prepared earlier, and the ushers had them available for the children, who agreed to help in this way.)*

Let us join together in a word of prayer: Our God, we thank you for giving us stones that can remind us of Jesus' coming into our lives. Help us each to shout out his love, and remind others of his presence for them. We thank you in his name. Amen. *(The children are then dismissed, and the organist plays some "traveling music" as they return to their seats.)*

Attitude

The attitude on this occasion was very positive and exceptionally festive. The occasion was the Palm Sunday service of worship (March 27, 1983); the sanctuary was well filled with people beginning to be caught up in the anticipation of Holy Week and Easter. The excitement of the time of year had been heightened by a number of planned Holy Week services in our community, including a cantata that the chancel choir of our congregation would be performing on Maundy Thursday. Good Friday and Easter services were also in the plans.

The children were well received this day, at least partially because of their participation in the opening of our service of worship (three of the children processed with the choir carrying palms for the chancel). This seemed to reinforce their sense of belonging and contribution to the worship of the congregation, and had a beneficial effect for both the children and the congregation as a whole.

My own attitude was positive. The Bible study groups and church membership classes I had led during Lent had been excellent, the various services scheduled for Holy Week were all looking very positive, the good attendance during the morning worship service for the day, the enthusiastic role of the children in the opening of worship, and the season itself all were encouraging experiences. The large number of children of all ages in the worship service, and some particularly good experiences with some of them during the days preceding this Sunday had made my attitude toward the children a good one.

Setting

The liturgical setting for the children's sermon was a prelude by the organist ("The Pastoral Symphony" from Handel's *Messiah*), a responsive call to worship composed of selections from Isaiah 52 and Isaiah 61 (found in *Christian Worship: A Hymnal*,[106] the Old Testament reading for Palm Sunday), two hymns—a processional hymn, "Crown Him with Many Crowns" and a hymn of prayer, "Beneath the Cross of Jesus" (which pointed the worshipers toward the passion of Christ), an invocation from *A Handbook for the Lectionary*,[107] based on the readings for Passion (Palm) Sunday, Year C, the reading of the assigned lessons, and a time of silent prayer followed by a pastoral prayer and a choral response.

The physical setting was more festive than usual, with the presence of the palms showing the dominance of this theme in the structure and direction of worship. Our congregation had recently installed the last of six memorial windows, and their addition to the sanctuary was a welcome one. The striking violet of the paraments for Holy Week added both a festive and a majestic tone to the experience.

Audience

Because Palm Sunday is traditionally one of the better-attended services of worship in this congregation, I anticipated a large number of children for the children's sermon. I was not aware of any major problems affecting the lives of the children I expected to be present for this worship experience.

I was aware of an increasing excitement among the children as Easter drew closer. The schools in the State of Alabama take a spring vacation during Holy Week, so many of the children and their families were preparing to leave town for a few days, adding to the excitement of the time. My knowledge of this fact created some uncertainty about the nature and size of the audience I could anticipate.

In the presentation of the children's sermon itself, there were approximately fifteen children participating. This was a slightly larger group than I had anticipated, given the school break. Those children in attendance were all very responsive and eager to participate. The involvement of some of their number in the opening of worship had given all of them a heightened sense of the sanctity of the chancel area as well as some personal ownership in the totality of the worship service.

The age distribution seemed relatively even, with a slight advantage to those children in the eight-to-ten-year category (Stage 2). There were no children present who were not in some way involved in the ongoing life of the congregation.

Content

This service of worship was given its thematic structure by two things: Palm Sunday and Holy Week. It became apparent that Palm Sunday needed to be held in relation to the entire experience of Holy Week, and this affected the way in which the Scriptures were read and interpreted. The appointed readings for this Palm Sunday—Year C in the Presbyterian, United Church of Christ, and Disciples lectionary were Isaiah 59:14–20; 1 Timothy 1:12–17; and Luke 19:28–40. Let us look more closely at the last of these three scriptures.

Luke shares the Synoptic description of the entry of Jesus into Jerusalem, following the Marcan form more closely than the Matthean. Like Mark, Luke lacks the specific reference to Zechariah 9:9 found in Matthew 21:5, although the general presentation of the triumphal entry into the city seems to assume this Messianic prediction.

The distinctive marks of the author are found in the closing verses (vs. 37–40). In the first instance (v. 37), the jubilant crowd giving witness to his entry becomes specifically defined as "the disciples," who rejoice because of his "mighty works." The second major alteration is in the content of the disciples' shout. "Hosanna" ("Save us, we implore you") is missing. Jesus is explicitly referred to as the "King who comes in the name of the Lord," and the clause, "Peace in heaven and glory in the highest" (reminiscent of the praise of the angels at the birth of Jesus in Luke 2:14) is added. The third distinctive feature is the mention in verses 39 and 40 of the inevitability of such a vocal witness to these mighty works: "I tell you, if these were silent, the very stones would cry out."

It is the third of these Lukan additions that is of particular interest. The reference to shouting or crying stones is, at best, an odd image. I. Howard Marshall lists four possible interpretations of the reference, and concludes, "In any case, the saying serves to underline the truth of the messianic acclamation in v. 38."[108] This truth, and its inevitable proclamation by disciples, crowds, or stones is, from Luke's perspective, the apparent point of the entire episode of Jesus' entry into the Holy City. The one who enters must be proclaimed Lord and king, and even the stones would bear witness to that fact, should the people not.

Toward a Theme. Because of the Palm Sunday setting of this set of lessons, the passage from Luke became the dominant reading, with the selections from Isaiah and 1 Timothy providing a helpful structure by which the Gospel lesson could be interpreted. The theme that emerged in the process came from the odd remark in Luke 19:40 concerning the stones "crying out." Both the Greek word *kraksousin* and its Hebrew equivalent refer to crying out in witness to something.[109] Thus the function of the stones in this passage is equivalent to the action of the disciples, as well as those who were sent ('*apostollon,* another distinctively Lukan reference found in v. 32). The stones therefore represent the ongoing, unstoppable proclamation of the identity and work of Christ.

Such a theme of proclamation as the imperative given by the triumphal entry is further reinforced in reference to Holy Week, where the impending absence of Jesus from the scene places the vocation of the disciples as his continuous voice in stark contrast to their silence on the night of betrayal. Luke understands the role of the church and the early founders of that body to be the continuation of the earthly ministry of Jesus, and the verbal and symbolic images of the Palm Sunday pericope give further confirmation of this theme. The continuity of the message proclaimed by Jesus is guaranteed by the witness of disciples and even by stones.

Form

The sermon that concluded the service of worship on this Palm Sunday and the earlier children's sermon both focused on the stones as images or symbols of our common calling to continue the unstoppable proclamation of the entry and work of Christ in the lives of individual Christians and of the body of Christ at large. Because Palm Sunday stands at the head of a week of special services, it seemed appropriate to attempt a tangible means of connecting Holy Week with Palm Sunday and Easter Sunday. I therefore used stones, which were given to each child and eventually to each worshiper, as a means of focusing on the image that was present in the text, tying together the three observances of the week, and providing a constant reminder of the message each time the children happened across the stone in the course of their

92

activities. The same stones were used the following Sunday, when they were compared with seeds, from which new life may spring. When these factors were all taken together, the object lesson form was the appropriate choice for the sermon.

Images

The object, a piece of gravel or stone, was itself an image of the inevitable proclamation of Christ. Instead of merely picturing a stone in their imaginations, the children were presented with an objective, tangible example of the almost preposterous claim of the gospel lesson. In this instance, the object served to move a difficult analogy out of the realm of the conceptual and into the tactile and visual fields which, when joined with the acoustic field, made the gospel image more appropriable.

A second image employed was one derived in part from the epistle lesson: these were not just stones; they became, in the course of the children's sermon, the possession of each child. Here Paul's conversion as a model for others who may have felt inadequate for ministry became pictured in the giftedness attached to the reception of the stones. The comments in the sermon about the varying sizes, shapes, and colors of the stones, as well as the choice of the insignificant gravel-type of stone were intended to reinforce this point.

Finally, the image of the stones in proclaiming the nature of Christ and one's relation to him was addressed in two ways. One, the suggestion that the stones be carried with the participants each day during the week and in all settings in those days of Holy Week intended to point to the ongoing nature of the proclamation. And the permanence of stones, particularly the one mentioned in the city park, was meant to point to the eternal nature of this proclamation.

Evaluation

The sermon was very well received by the children, who seemed to have been particularly attentive. The fact that the object was not something completely external to themselves (such as a picture of a monument stone or a flannel graph with some characters), but was something they each held helped to communicate the theme I was trying to utilize. Because the stones were something familiar placed in a fresh light, I felt they served well as pedagogical devices.

The children evidently heard something of what was said in the sermon—a good number of them returned the following Sunday with their stones. I had anticipated that those who did follow this request would be primarily the older children, and this was in fact the case. I had prepared more gravel for the sermon on Easter Sunday for those who had forgotten to bring theirs. This suggestion helped to make the experience from Palm Sunday to Easter a unified one.

Theologically, the children were renewing their memories of Christ and what he had taught each time they experienced the stones. The similarity between such an objective function of a memorial of Christ and the significance of the anamnesis function of the Lord's Supper is striking. The children were essentially charged with allowing an external object to recreate an internal experience by means of the memory.

Because of the limitations of their ages, the children involved could not be expected to grasp the deeper conceptual intricacies of Luke's "stones of witness." They could, however, experience their own stones, given them as means of remembering Christ during a very special week, and allowing those stones to "speak" a message to them each time they came in contact with them. It may well be that children can accept "shouting stones" more easily than we.

The fact that the children assisted in passing the gravel to the congregation following the children's sermon helped to pull the experiences of the children and the congregation together. There was a great sense of interdependence that day, and the objects—small, insignificant pieces of gravel—helped to unify the service of worship and the experience of the Holy Week in a special way.[110]

Drama or Participatory Story: "The Wall"

(Genesis 1:1–5; Ephesians 2:11–18; Luke 3:15–17, 21–22)

(As the children gather in the chancel area and take their seats on the floor close to the preacher, he or she welcomes each one, informally, warmly and sincerely. Once each child is settled, the children's sermon begins.)

I need your help today. First, let's all stand up, so we can move around more easily. *(The children stand, and titter a bit as they do so.)* Now, let's put some of you here *(take three or four of the children by the shoulders and move them to the preacher's right)*, some of you here *(move another few to the preacher's left)*, and leave the rest of you right here in the middle *(places these children in single file)*. OK! Good!

Now, those of you in the middle, I want you to link arms together like this. *(Demonstrate with one of the children by linking right elbow with left elbow so those in the middle form a chain or a wall; this activity produces giggles and a few reluctant participants.)* Make it a good strong link, because I want you to be a wall *(make sure the wall is perpendicular to the chancel steps)*, and what I want that wall to do is to keep the people on this side *(point to the children on the right)* from reaching the people on this side *(point to the children on the left; as the children realize the "game," there is more giggling and some fidgeting.)*

Now, you other two groups *(addressing each one in turn)*, I want you to try to reach each other, but with one rule: you can't go **around** the wall *(the pronunciation of the rule was accompanied by groans and an audible "Darn!")* You'll have to pretend that the ends of this wall go as far as you can see. OK? All right, begin. *(The preacher should maintain order and not let the situation get out of hand. Thirty seconds would be plenty of time for this activity, which was accompanied by much laughter and motion.)*

OK, calm down for a moment. Now *(addressing the children who have been separated by the wall)*, what does it feel like to be kept apart like that? *(Allow a few seconds for responses from the children, and acknowledge the feelings expressed by repeating them and affirming them. The children who participated in this sermon used such terms as "frustrating," and "I didn't like it.")* Yes, it makes us frustrated and a little bit angry to be kept apart, doesn't it? *(Acknowledge the heads nodding in the affirmative.)*

Travis, will you come here for a moment? *(Choose one of the children from either side of the wall.)* I want you to go up to the wall, place your hands on one of the places where two of the children have locked arms *(allow him to do so),* and very gently help them separate their arms *(the children who form the wall had to be encouraged to let go!)* Good! Now you folks on either side can go ahead and shake each other's hands, or hug each other, or whatever! *(Allow a few seconds for this; the children may need some encouragement here as well.)*

Let's sit back down here now. *(After the children are settled once again, proceed with the sermon.)* There are lots of things that try real hard to keep people apart, like the wall you just made, and that's frustrating. Sometimes it's the color of our skin, our age, the part of the country we live in, or even the fact that we live in different countries. There's a wall between us, so we're kept apart, just like you were.

The Bible verses I read earlier reflect the fact that God gets frustrated with these walls too! In fact, the passage from Ephesians says that God grew so frustrated with those walls of prejudice, mistrust, and hatred that Jesus was sent to tear up and break down those walls, just like Travis did here.

The walls that separate us from each other also keep us from doing what God would have us do. That's why God sent Christ to break down the tough walls that are a part of human nature. But God also gave us the job of breaking down the walls we can get at. If we don't, they may never get broken down, and we may never get to know what it's like to know each other and to love God.

Let us pray: God, help us break down those walls that keep us apart from each other and from you. Make us people who act like Jesus to destroy those walls. Amen.

Attitude

The attitude on this occasion was positive, if a bit confusing. Because this Sunday came at the end of the first week of school after the Christmas break, those present seemed a bit uncertain and uneasy. The return to a schedule of activity in the weekday from the relative freedom of vacation time seemed to have the congregation off center.

The attendance at worship, which traditionally dips for the Sundays immediately following Christmas Day, was at the normal level for

96

the winter months. The community had experienced no major traumas and the congregation was fairly stable in its common life.

The children were obviously tired from their Christmas break and the return to the school routine. On this particular Sunday there were two visiting children who participated in the children's sermon. Their presence contributed some uneasiness to the situation, but most of the "regular attenders" seemed quite willing to include these two in their midst.

My own attitude was, at best, a little depressed. December had been a difficult month, personally and professionally, for me. My own vacation time had been hampered by the necessity of returning for worship on January 2, and I was still feeling that frustration. The presence of a sizable crowd in worship on this Sunday, and particularly of a young family of visitors, helped to lift my spirits.

Setting

The liturgical setting was determined by the designation of this as First Sunday After the Epiphany—Year C. Our denomination, as well as our particular congregation, remains somewhat unaware of any but the major church seasons, so the significance of Epiphany as a season for "strengthening human relationships in the light of the Gospel" (as our Church Program Guide expresses it) was something that required conscious action on the part of those who plan and program church activities. In the "Worship Notes" our congregation publishes at the beginning of each season, I had attempted to begin educating the congregation to this emphasis.

The lectionary readings for this Sunday were unique to the tradition the Disciples share with the Presbyterian Churches and the United Church of Christ. Only the Gospel lesson corresponded to the four other common lectionaries. Another difference was our lack of designating the First Sunday After the Epiphany as "The Baptism of Our Lord," as is the case in most other church bodies.

The call to worship on this Sunday was taken from *Christian Worship: A Service Book,* and was a combination of Psalm 43:3 and Isaiah 58:8, both of which deal with the sending out of God's light, and its role in healing and righteousness.[111] The invocation was the Collect assigned for this Sunday and its texts in *A Handbook for the Lectionary,* and reflected the theme of all three lessons.[112] The two hymns preceding the children's sermon were Beethoven & Van Dyke's "Joyful, Joyful, We Adore Thee" for the hymn of praise (in which verse 1 ends, "Fill us with the light of day"), and the Hymn of Prayer attempted to tie together the themes of the Light of the world and the ministry of reconciliation.

The physical setting was standard, the only real change being the presence of the white paraments. Because of the cool temperatures the children were warmly clothed, and this restricted their movement somewhat.

Audience

I had anticipated a small group of children to be present for this service of worship and prepared accordingly. The fact that the children were just returning to school from a long Christmas break and the traditionally slight attendance at worship on the first few Sundays after Christmas seemed to indicate that we could expect to have six to eight children present and participating in the children's sermon. The group I anticipated were basically the steady "core group" of children who attend practically every Sunday.

The sermon I originally planned was based on no more than eight children, with four of the children in the middle forming the wall, and two children on each side. I felt a bit uncomfortable with these numbers but planned the sermon with this in mind.

As the sermon was actually conducted, there were more than a dozen children participating, including the two new children (a brother and sister), whom the other children did not know. This created the necessity of altering the sermon a bit to accommodate both the larger numbers and the presence of two uncertain and unknown children.

The children present for the sermon were more affected by the presence of their two new friends than by anything else in the service. They were excited but still somewhat hesitant about these visitors. The planned use of the "wall of separation" theme was fortunate, given the altered circumstances of the day. The "wall" of strangeness was as operative as the one in the sermon and helped the children experience the issue of reconciliation more personally as they came to participate together in the exercise.

Content

The lectionary texts assigned for the day were Genesis 1:1–5; Ephesians 2:11–18; and Luke 3:15–17, 21–22.

The governing theme of the Letter to the Ephesians, the vision of the universality of the church, is given two of its most distinctive images in Chapter 2. The first, found in the passage for this Sunday, is that of Christ functioning to break down the "dividing wall of hostility" between Gentiles and Jews (vs. 13–16). The second is that of the church as a building with a "foundation of the apostles and prophets" and Christ as the "cornerstone" (vs. 19–22).

The reference to the "dividing wall of hostility" is generally agreed to refer to the construction of the temple in Jerusalem, which had the central sanctuary surrounded by a series of courts, each of which was walled in order to separate those admitted from those excluded. The outermost of these courts was called the Court of the Gentiles, and no non-Jew could go beyond its walls, under penalty of death for the trespasser. In light of the reference to the ritual differences between the Gentiles and the Jews in v. 11 (uncircumcision vs. circumcision), it would seem that these suggestions about the analogy between these "dividing walls" and the temple walls might be correct.

The point of our passage is that in Christ those walls that separate people have been destroyed, and the Jew and the Greek have been reconciled once and for all. Because of his reconciling ministry, those who were afar off have been brought near to God, and all human enmity must also cease, "for through him we both have access in one Spirit to the Father" (v. 18). That which had separated was now opened up.

Toward a Theme. In light of the liturgical setting of the three lessons for this Sunday within the general Epiphany theme of "strengthening human relationships," the focus of the lessons seems to be directed toward the passage from Ephesians, with the Old Testament and Gospel readings helping to inform that Epistle reading. The common theme that emerged from the scripture was separation (of light, of people, of the heavens) and the role of God's reconciling acts, culminating in Jesus Christ, in overcoming the separation of people from each other and from God.

For the sermon that concluded the day's worship, this theme was addressed with the title, "The Light: Divided and Spread," and emphasized that the division of light and the other acts of Creation were so that this same light might be spread more effectively. Using the analogy of a laser, which separates light into its component parts and isolates and intensifies one color to incredible strength, the sermon brought in the other two readings to illustrate the role of Christ in intensifying the reconciling work of God, particularly in destroying those things that continue to separate us.

In developing the children's sermon, speculation about lasers and the separation of light seemed both too technical and too abstract. I therefore focused on the object of Christ's reconciling ministry according to this material: "The dividing wall of hostility" in Ephesians 2:14.

Form

Instead of merely talking about a wall between people that separates them, or using a picture of a wall to illustrate the point, it seemed more appropriate in this situation to allow the children to become the wall and the people separated by it. By becoming the wall, some of the children involved in the children's sermon could experience themselves as obstacles to the attempts of others to unite with each other, while the other children could experience the frustration of being locked out of fellowship by this obstacle. The appropriate form to communicate this experience emerged as drama or participatory story.

Images

The predominant image was the one taken from the text of Ephesians 2:14—the wall. But it was not sufficient to simply build a wall, since the function of the wall referred to in the passage was to increase the alienation of people (specifically Gentiles and Jews) from each other. The simple image of the wall was therefore transformed in the following ways.

By having one group of children become the wall of division and separation, the image of the wall was changed from the conceptual realm to the experiential. It became not only a tangible reality, but one that some children who participated experienced as something that they did. At least a portion of the theme presented by the lectionary readings was the role of persons in building these dividing walls, and the children who made the wall this day were imaging this reality. Their natural tendency not to let the other groups past their space or into their territory enabled those children to experience the role they might have in creating walls in their own relationships.

The process of being separated from each other arbitrarily also helped the other children to experience alienation and the frustration of their attempts to overcome the obstacle of the wall. The growing sense of frustration was obvious as the situation progressed.

The role of the one child (Travis) in separating the wall so the two sides could commune was the third transformation of the wall as a sole image. It was obvious to me and to most adults that this child was the Christ figure, and this image was picked up by some of the older children as well. The inclusion of this image in the children's sermon was a response to the two New Testament readings and their assessment of the function of Christ in God's reconciling work. But a further image was also presented: one was chosen from within their midst, adopted if you will, for this purpose. Thus, the children could begin to see themselves as those who break down walls.

100

Evaluation

The choice of the "participatory story" form for this sermon allowed several things to happen. One, it provided the children a sense of freedom and movement lacking in a story, lecture, or sermon. The necessity of moving from one place to another, of physically dividing themselves into different groups, and of engaging in a specific action gave the children a sense of involvement and engagement in the sermon rather than mere speculative hearing of it. The inclusion of movement and action, always characteristic of this form of children's sermon, appeals to the needs of children in Stages 1 and 2.

This form also allowed to emerge a sense of common work. Those children who became the wall quickly accepted the challenge of keeping the other children apart. They also learned that they must work together to do this. Likewise, the children on either side of the wall soon discovered that they would have a better chance of succeeding in their tasks with a common effort than with solo attacks on the wall, and they began organizing themselves informally along those lines. My comments to the children did not reflect this emphasis as much as the action itself did.

A further contribution this form made to the sermon was the ease of including the visiting children in this common work. The theological work of reconciliation was more clearly demonstrated in their inclusion in this common action and the acceptance of their contributions by the other children involved than any number of well-chosen words could have accomplished.

The sermon itself could have dealt more directly with the Christ-figure role of the chosen child at the end of the experiential portion of the sermon. One problem of this form is that it takes more time to set up the action and ensure that the children know their roles than the time of the actual drama. When the action had been completed, I felt pressed for time and probably short-changed the movement to reflection and interpretation I needed to make.

Story: "Two Rowdy Boys"

(2 Samuel 12:1–7a; Galatians 2:15–21; Luke 7:36–50)

(As the children gather and are taking their seats on the floor close to the preacher, he or she welcomes them informally, both verbally and nonverbally, greeting the children by name when possible. Once the children are settled, he or she begins.)

My neighbor, Mr. Franz, had two of his nephews visit him recently. John, who was nine years old, and Jay, who was six, had come for a few weeks while their parents were away on a business trip. Now Mr. Franz had been excited about the visit because he had never had any children of his own, although he loved them dearly. His favorite companion seemed to be his puppy, on whom he lavished all kinds of gifts, love, and attention. He was happy to be having such fine young boys with him.

But there was a problem: the boys were terribly rowdy, and not too happy about being at their uncle's place without their parents. So they looked for mischief to get into, and when children look for mischief, they can usually find it.

Jay, the younger boy, began with the cookie jar, from which he stole some cookies and then accidentally knocked over the cookie jar and broke it. Then he ran so hard against the screen door going outside that he knocked a hole in the screen. And, finally, in digging in the dirt, he managed to dig up some of Mr. Franz' pretty flowers.

John was doing different things from his brother, but was being just as rowdy. First, while throwing rocks in the back yard, he broke a window; then while running to the refrigerator, he knocked over a lamp in the living room and broke it. But worst of all, as he played with his uncle's puppy, he played so roughly with it that the puppy died. *(The faces of the children fell at this statement!)*

When Mr. Franz came home, the signs of their rowdiness and mischief were everywhere. He was hurt and disappointed in the way his two nephews had behaved while he was away. So, after he had surveyed

102

the damage and made arrangements for his puppy, he called John and Jay in to see him.

They were terrified! They were convinced they were in awful trouble and knew they would be punished for the things they had done wrong. But you know what? Mr. Franz looked right at both of them and said, "Boys, you've disappointed me and hurt my feelings, but I forgive you for what you've done. I ask only that you help me pay for the damage you've done, and that you promise to think about this before you do any more mischief."

(Then a question is put to the children) Now, which of these two boys do you think was the most grateful to the uncle? *(Allow some moments for reaction, then conclude.)* Sins are those things we do to other people, to plants and animals, and to God that could break even the love of a relative for us. But we've got a God who forgives our sins, even when there are lots of them, even when they are awful things. God doesn't say that they are not sins, but God doesn't allow those things to keep us separated from the kingdom of God. Instead, we are given the opportunity to turn our lives around and live the life God would prefer.

Let us pray: Our God, we thank you that you are a forgiving God, and that you don't hold the rowdy things we do against us. Forgive us when we sin against you and your creatures. Amen. *(The children are then dismissed and the organist plays some "traveling music" as they return to their seats.)*

Attitude

The prevailing mood on this occasion was festive. School was out for the summer, church camps were being readied, and preparations were being made for Father's Day, which was the following Sunday. Because children's sermons had been a regular part of our worship services for four years, the congregation had come to expect a good experience with them and listened intently to the story. Congregational acceptance of the children's presence in worship has increased steadily over the years.

The children have come to anticipate this experience, and more of them now stay for the entire service of worship than before. It has become a helpful means of integrating children of new families into the life of the church as well!

My own attitude on this day was upbeat. I felt good about the service of worship, and particularly the two sermons I had prepared, so the story flowed easily. There were eight children present, as I recall, so eye contact was possible with each, and my relationship with each child had been positive.

Setting

The story was prepared liturgically by the selection of a call to worship based around the central theme of the service: God's forgiveness of sinners. The two hymns that preceded the story were "Come, Thou Almighty King," which invokes God's blessing of the people and a Spirit of holiness, and "I Am Thine, Lord," with its themes of approaching the cross of Christ in response to the word of grace. The invocation was taken from *A Handbook for the Lectionary*.[113] The pastoral prayer, which immediately preceded the story, tied in thematically with both the readings and the concerns and needs of the congregation and the community.

The physical setting remains fairly constant. I sit on the bottom step at the entry to the chancel and the children gather on the floor in a semicircle in front of me. With the church in the Pentecost season, the green paraments are dominant. The physical setting is comfortable, with carpeting on the floors. The children are close enough to me, to each other, and to the chancel and its triple images of Word (Bible and sermon), communion, and baptism (Disciples use immersion, so a baptistry is present) to have a powerful effect upon them.

Audience

The audience for the children's sermon this day was eight children, fairly evenly divided by sex, between the ages of five and nine. I was not aware of any emotional trauma affecting the lives of the children present. The major issue in the community including the church was the onset of summer vacation, and all the children were affected by that.

It became obvious to me that the audience for the children's sermon would know a lot about sin and forgiveness, but not in those terms. On this issue the conceptual differences in development between adults and children were acute. So, rather than address the issue to the audience on the level of **concepts** of sin and forgiveness, I chose to address it experientially. What child has not mischievously broken a window or hurt a pet and then felt remorse and sorrow at this "sin"?

The children were eager to participate this day, and this fed me as I presented the story. The relationship between us was an especially warm one as we shared in this parable of "Two Rowdy Boys."

Content

The service of worship was governed by its location in the church year. It was the Fifth Sunday After Pentecost—Year C, with the lectionary texts 2 Samuel 12:1–7a; Galatians 2:15–21; and Luke 7:36–50.

104

Let us take a closer look at Luke 7:36–50. Luke takes the story of the "Woman with the Ointment," which he shares with the other three Gospels (although John's version is a conflation of this story, the story of Mary and Martha, and the story of the defection of Judas) and makes two startling changes. The first is Luke's placement of the story following his "Sermon on the Plain" (Luke 6:20–49) and two other stories and a dialogue (the centurion's slave and the widow's son at Nain, plus the dialogue with John's disciples concerning Jesus' identity), all of which are commentaries on the closing statement of the sermon concerning "hearers and doers of the word." This is a radically different setting from that of Matthew 26:6–13 and Mark 14:3–9, where the story stands at the beginning of the Passion Narrative. In the First and Second Gospels, the act of anointing is interpreted to be a preparation for burial, in anticipation of his coming death. In Luke's context, the woman anoints his feet with her tears, fulfilling the role of a servant and showing her desperate love for him.

The second major departure in Luke's text is the insertion of verses 40–43, the parable of the two debtors, which he uses to illustrate what constitutes forgiveness of sins. Jesus' host has become preoccupied by the reputation of the woman and cannot see the significance of her act or of Jesus' subsequent act of forgiving her sins. The parable sets up a dichotomy between two debtors, one with larger debts than the other, who are both forgiven of their debts by the creditor. The question to the Pharisee, "Which of them will love him more?" is, like the parable of the ewe lamb in 2 Samuel 12, so designed that there is only one possible answer, and the Pharisee is thus convicted of his own lack of understanding. A story which, in its other Synoptic setting was an introduction to, and possibly a warrant for, the Passion Narrative, has now been transformed into a story about true discipleship and the forgiveness of sins.

Toward a Theme. The major theme that emerged from the readings was the role of the parable or the gospel in revealing oneself as a sinner against one's neighbor, one's God, and oneself, along with the startling fact of the gospel lesson that God forgives the repentant sinner no matter how horrible the sin.

In the sermon at the conclusion of the service, the emphasis was placed on the commonality of sin. Simon the Pharisee was suggested as the appropriate analogy for the average person in the pew. His sin was that of smugness in rebuking the sins of others while allowing his own sins to go unchallenged. The brief parable of the two debtors reminds us that **both** persons owe debts and that both are forgiven those debts, a message Simon and the average Christian both need to hear.

In the children's sermon, the approach to this controlling theme would be somewhat limited by the "appropriability" of the concept of sin, as indicated earlier. The decision to reflect the same general theme, presented by the content of the lectionary readings, in both sermons required a consideration of the experiential level at which children could see themselves revealed as both sinners and as forgiven sinners. The segment of the lessons for the day that seemed to reveal this most clearly was the parable of the two debtors in Luke 7:41–42. Here the common human experience of sin is represented in its variety and in inevitable terms. The choice of two debtors, both of whom owe the creditor, provides the children with two characters with whom to identify, and the choice given Simon by Jesus in response to the parable allows the children to enter into the parable.

Form

Because two out of the three passages in the lessons utilized the parable form, along with narrative, it seemed appropriate to adopt the same form for this children's sermon. Thus, a story was developed in which two boys experienced a similar relationship with their uncle as that of the two debtors with the creditor in Luke's parable. The story form communicates the same invitation to personal involvement with the experiences of the characters as that implicit in the parables in 2 Samuel 12 and Luke 7. "Story" seems to be almost demanded as the most appropriate way of presenting the complex issue of sin to children in a way that will communicate both the essence of human sinfulness and their own experience of that sinfulness. Parables are forms that have been proven effective in communicating these same issues. Therefore, the story form was chosen.

Images

Because children can see themselves more clearly reflected in the activities of other children and animals, the first decision was to make the two debtors of the parable in Luke two rowdy young boys. I chose to make the two children ages (6 and 9) that placed the characters in two different stages of development (end of Stage 1 and middle of Stage 2) in order to engage the children present for the children's sermon in a person who thought and acted as they did. I also chose to make these characters related to the adult in the story in order to heighten the sense of responsibility the children should feel to him. Each character was named, because children in these two stages are less able to generalize than to particularize. Names make the characters real. Instead of talk-

106

ing about children and relatives in general, we were thus engaged in a story about John, Jay, and their uncle, Mr. Franz.

The action of the story itself was designed to accomplish the same thing as the Lukan parable. But, because children would not relate well to owing money to someone, the prevailing image of the parable of the two debtors, I chose an alternate image, based on a combination of the image of the ewe lamb in 2 Samuel 12 and that of the sinful woman in the Gospel.

Both the children were presented as committing sins or transgressions against their uncle. Their specific acts, such as stealing cookies, breaking a window, and ruining a screen door, were chosen for their universality in the experience of children. These acts were the "hook" designed to engage the children in the action and experience of the story. I also tried to make the "sins" of the older boy more despicable than those of the younger, as a means of introducing the question asked Simon about the two debtors, "Which one of them will love him more?" I added the event of the death of the puppy to illustrate the serious nature of the older boy's sins in comparison with those of the younger boy, to relate to the image of the killing of the ewe lamb in Nathan's parable, and to appeal to the sense of fairness and respect for life that characterizes children of these stages.

The first image is of a parental figure (who is not exactly a parent to the children) forgiving both children for the wrong they had done to him. Although both had "sinned" against him, and although there was a great difference between the nature of the types of sin (the equivalent of five hundred denarii compared to fifty in the respective debts), the uncle's forgiveness was given to both on an equal basis. The issue, as in Luke's parable, was shifted to the gratitude one feels for unmerited forgiveness of sins, and the unnamed woman could therefore become a person with whom the children could relate.

Evaluation

The children reacted to the story with a high degree of attention and involvement. As I came to the statement about the uncle's puppy dying, the faces of the children reflected a sorrow and engagement that said the point had registered.

When, at the end of the story, I asked, "Now, which of these two boys do you think was the most grateful to the uncle?" the responses were immediate and unanimous: John, the elder nephew. When I asked, "Why?" the unanimous response was, "Because he killed the puppy, and that is a lot worse than stealing cookies!" The response to this children's sermon was very spontaneous and active, which indicated I had struck a nerve for those involved.

I felt the children who comprised the audience that Sunday had had a chance to see themselves in the actions of these two children, had come to experience their own sins in the process, and had experienced both the existence of differences in the severity of those sins and the enormous gift of forgiveness in relation to that universal human condition.

Notes

1. Anthony Towne, *Excerpts from the Diaries of the Late God*. Harper and Row, Publishers, 1968. p. 50.
2. Stan Stewart, "R-Rated Worship." *Thesis Theological Cassettes*, Vol. 10 (May 1979).
3. Charles R. Foster, *Teaching in the Community of Faith*. Abingdon Press, 1982. p. 17.
4. John H. Westerhoff, III, *Bringing Up Children in the Christian Faith*. Winston Press, Inc., 1980. p. 24. He repeats an image used earlier in *Will Our Children Have Faith?* which compares the development of children's faith to that of a tree, which adds rings to its "treeness" each year.
5. David Ng and Virginia Thomas, *Children in the Worshiping Community*. John Knox Press, 1981. p. 18.
6. G. R. Beasley-Murray, "A Baptist Interpretation of the Place of the Child in the Church." *Foundations*, Vol. 8 (April 1965), p. 147.
7. Philip W. McLarty, *The Children, Yes! Involving Children in Our Congregation's Worship*. Discipleship Resources, 1981. p. 28. Emphasis added is mine.
8. Foster, *Teaching in the Community of Faith*. p. 65.
9. Westerhoff, *Bringing Up Children in the Christian Faith*. p. 18.
10. Jerome W. Berryman, "Being in Parables with Children." *Religious Education*, Vol. 74 (May–June 1979), p. 272.
11. Ibid., p. 273.
12. Westerhoff, *Bringing Up Children in the Christian Faith*. p. 19.
13. Foster, *Teaching in the Community of Faith*. p. 61.
14. David R. Hunter, *Christian Education as Engagement*. Seabury Press, 1963. p. 11.
15. Ibid., p. 16.
16. Ibid., p. 7, where Hunter describes "engagement" as "meeting, knowing (not knowing about), responding to or ignoring, loving, hating . . . As a theological term, then *engagement* is the moment when God acts in or upon the life of an individual and the individual faces the obligation to respond."
17. Walter J. Harrelson, "Children in the Church." *Foundations*, Vol. 11 (April 1963), p. 145.
18. See especially Erik Erikson, "Identity and the Life Cycle." *Psychological Issues*, Vol. 1, No. 1 (1959); Jean Piaget, *Six Psychological Studies*. Random House, Vintage Books, 1967; or "Piaget's Theory," *Carmichael's Manual of Child Psychology*, Vol. 1, third edition. John Wiley and Sons, 1970. A better option, in light of Piaget's extensive and technical work, might be Herbert Ginsberg and Sylvia Opper, *Piaget's Theory of Intellectual Development*. Prentice Hall, 1969. Kohlberg's theory is most accessible in Lawrence Kohlberg, "Stages of Moral Development as a Basis for Moral Education," *Moral Education: Interdisciplinary Approaches,* ed. C. M. Beck, B. S. Crittenden, and E. V. Sullivan. Newman Press, 1971. pp. 23–93. An imaginative contribution to seeing the interrelatedness of the three approaches to human psychological development as it relates to faith has been made by James W. Fowler, *Stages of Faith: The Psychology of Human Development and the Quest for Meaning*. Harper & Row, Publishers, 1981. See especially Part III, pp. 37–86.
19. Fowler, *Stages of Faith*. p. 64.
20. Erikson, "Identity and the Life Cycle." pp. 52ff.
21. Ibid., p. 57.

22. James W. Fowler, "Perspectives on the Family from the Standpoint of Faith Development Theory." *Perkins School of Theology Journal,* Vol. 33 (Fall 1979), p. 7.

23. James W. Fowler, "Toward a Developmental Perspective on Faith." *Religious Education,* Vol. 69 (March–April 1974), p. 207.

24. Fowler, *Stages of Faith.* See especially Chapter 23 and the section entitled, "Conversion, Sponsorship and the Recapitulation of Previous Stages," pp. 286–291.

25. Erikson, "Identity and the Life Cycle." p. 56.

26. Ibid.

27. Ibid., pp. 64–65.

28. Lucie W. Barber, "Ministry with Parents of Infants and Preschool Children." *Religious Education,* Vol. 69 (March–April 1974), p. 194. She claims, "Most religious educators will agree that what the baby learns, what the child senses, about his parents' love and concern is ultimately related to adult understanding of a loving God." See also Edward W. Pohlman, "Infant Experience and Human Belief About Ultimate Causes." *The Journal of Pastoral Care,* Vol. 19 (Spring 1965), p. 28, and Melanie Klein, "Our Adult World and Its Roots in Infancy." *Human Relations,* Vol. 12 (1959), pp. 291–303.

29. Fowler, *Stages of Faith.* p. 134.

30. Westerhoff, *Bringing Up Children in the Christian Faith.* pp. 25–26.

31. Kohlberg, "Stages of Moral Development." pp. 86–87.

32. Erikson, "Identity and the Life Cycle." p. 86.

33. Kohlberg, "Stages of Moral Development," p. 87.

34. C. Ellis Nelson, *Where Faith Begins.* John Knox Press, 1971. pp. 102ff.

35. Ibid., pp. 104–114.

36. Iris V. Cully, *Christian Worship and Church Education.* The Westminster Press, 1967. p. 11.

37. Donald E. Miller, "The Moral Significance of Worship." *Religious Education,* Vol. 75 (March–April 1980), p. 202.

38. Ng and Thomas, *Children in the Worshiping Community.* p. 140.

39. Amos Niven Wilder, Foreword to *Grace Confounding: Poems* by Amos N. Wilder. Fortress Press, 1972. p. ix.

40. Horace Bushnell, *Christian Nurture,* cited by Philip W. McLarty, *The Children, Yes!* Discipleship Resources, 1981. p. 36.

41. Ibid.

42. William H. Willimon, "The Relationship of Liturgical Education to Worship Participation." *Religious Education,* Vol. 69 (September–October 1974), pp. 621–627.

43. Cully, "Pastors as Teachers." *Religious Education,* Vol. 74 (March–April 1979), p. 122ff.

44. McLarty, *The Children, Yes!* p. 39.

45. Elise Shoemaker and Doris Willis, "Experiencing Worship with Children." Workers with Children Series. Discipleship Resources, undated pamphlet. p. 2. Shoemaker and Willis state: "Words have meaning for children only as they can relate them to some experience or physical reality within their understanding. Love has meaning only as a child experiences love from another person. God can be experienced as loving, caring, forgiving only as the child experiences relationships with persons who love, care and forgive."

46. Richard Avery and Donald Marsh, *The Avery and Marsh Songbook.* Proclamation Productions, Inc., song copyright 1972. p. 32.

47. Miller, "Moral Significance of Worship." p. 201.

48. Roger A. and Gertrude G. Gobbel, "Children and Worship." *Religious Education,* Vol. 74 (November–December 1979), p. 574.

49. Shoemaker and Willis, "Experiencing Worship with Children." p. 5.

50. Westerhoff, *Bringing Up Children in the Christian Faith.* p. 29.

51. Charles R. Foster, "Proclaiming the Word with Children." *Worship Alive*. Discipleship Resources, undated pamphlet. p. 5.

52. I have presented but a few of the contributions made to worship by the presence of children. For fuller discussion of this issue, the reader is referred to Foster, "Proclaiming"; Shoemaker and Willis, "Experiencing Worship with Children"; and Willimon, "Keep Them in Their Place?" All three are brief, accessible (through Discipleship Resources), and well argued.

53. Charles R. Stinette, Jr., "The Origin of the Symbolic Process." *The Journal of Pastoral Care*, Vol. 16 (Spring 1962), p. 15.

54. Gobbel and Gobbel, "Children and Worship." p. 572.

55. Berryman, "Being in Parables with Children." p. 284.

56. Richard Coleman, *Gospel-Telling: The Art and Theology of Children's Sermons.* William B. Eerdmans Publishing Company, 1982; Philip W. McLarty, *The Children, Yes!* Discipleship Resources, 1981; and James A. Carr, "The Children's Sermon: An Act of Worship for the Community of Faith." *The Perkins School of Theology Journal,* Vol. 36 (Spring 1983), pp. 1–57.

57. McLarty, *The Children, Yes!* pp. 1–2.

58. Willimon, "Keep Them in Their Place?" *Worship Alive*. Discipleship Resources, undated pamphlet, p. 5.

59. Ng and Thomas, *Children in the Worshiping Community*. p. 43; Foster, "Proclaiming the Word with Children," p. 2.

60. Willimon, "Keep Them in Their Place?" p. 5.

61. Westerhoff, *Bringing Up Children in the Christian Faith*. pp. 20, 42–43.

62. Ng and Thomas, *Children in the Worshiping Community*. p. 43.

63. Coleman, *Gospel-Telling*. pp. 30–31.

64. Ibid., p. 32.

65. Foster, "Proclaiming the Word with Children." p. 2.

66. Willimon, "Keep Them in Their Place?" p. 5.

67. Foster, "Proclaiming the Word with Children," p. 2.

68. Ng and Thomas, *Children in the Worshiping Community*. p. 43.

69. Willimon, "Keep Them in Their Place?" p. 5; Foster, "Proclaiming the Word with Children," p. 2.

70. Willimon, "Keep Them in Their Place?" p. 5.

71. Foster, "Proclaiming the Word with Children," p. 2 presents an argument reflective of Paulo Freire in *Pedagogy of the Oppressed*. Herder & Herder, 1972. pp. 58 passim.

72. Ng and Thomas, *Children in the Worshiping Community*. p. 43.

73. Foster, "Proclaiming the Word with Children." p. 2.

74. Willimon, "Keep Them in Their Place?" p. 5.

75. Gobbel and Gobbel, "Children and Worship." p. 572.

76. Coleman, *Gospel-Telling*. p. 15, suggests that a reasonable alternative to making three or four points in a children's sermon "is to carefully construct the proclamation so that it can be effective at more than one level . . . construct the sermon (situation) so that older children and adults can intuitively perceive a certain richness which they can pursue later."

77. Ibid., pp. 12–13.

78. Jack L. Seymour and Carol A. Wehrheim, "Faith Seeking Understanding: Interpretation as a Task of Christian Education." in *Contemporary Approaches to Christian Education,* ed. Jack L. Seymour and Donald E. Miller. Abingdon Press, 1982. p. 40, state "The Church as the company of pilgrims in search of meaning and vocation becomes the context for educational ministry."

79. Fred R. Craddock, *Overhearing the Gospel: Preaching and Teaching the Faith to Those Who Have Already Heard*. Abingdon Press, 1978.

80. Andrew J. Weaver, "Children's Sermons Are Fun." *The Christian Ministry,* Vol. 10 (July 1979), p. 23.

81. Berryman, "Being in Parables with Children." pp. 271–285.

82. Sallie McFague, *Speaking in Parables: A Study in Metaphor and Theology.* Fortress Press, 1975.

83. Westerhoff, "Of Liturgy and Learning." *Thesis Theological Cassettes,* Vol. 9 (May 1978).

84. Carr, "The Children's Sermon: An Act of Worship." pp. 9–10.

85. Ibid., pp. 23–24. "Succession of 'fixes' " is a phrase Carr quoted from Walter J. Ong, *The Presence of the Word.* Yale University Press, 1967. p. 129.

86. Erikson, "Identity and the Life Cycle." especially his introductory section, pp. 50–55.

87. Miller, "The Developmental Approach to Christian Education." in *Contemporary Approaches to Christian Education,* ed. Jack L. Seymour and Donald E. Miller. Abingdon Press, 1982. p. 88.

88. Carr, "The Children's Sermon: An Act of Worship." p. 33 passim, places the upper end of the audience for children's sermons at eight years.

89. Maria Harris, "The Original Vision: Children and Religious Experience." in *Family Ministry,* ed. Gloria Durka and Joanmarie Smith. Winston Press, 1980. p. 61.

90. Ibid., pp. 62ff.

91. McFague, *Speaking in Parables.* p. 139.

92. Coleman, McLarty, Carr, and many others share this belief.

93. See also Carr, "The Children's Sermon." pp. 26–28, who lists eight steps in his preparatory process.

94. Coleman, *Gospel-Telling.* pp. 14–15.

95. Seymour and Wehrheim, "Faith Seeking Understanding." p. 127.

96. Coleman, *Gospel-Telling.* p. 24.

97. Gerhard von Rad, *The Message of the Prophets.* Harper & Row, Publishers, 1965. p. 20.

98. Berryman, "Being in Parables with Children." p. 275.

99. Foster, "Proclaiming the Word with Children." pp. 3–5.

100. Dennis Lippart, "What About the Children's Sermon?" *The Church School.* Discipleship Resources, undated pamphlet. p. 20. Lippart presents a number of additional forms.

101. Martin Bell, *The Way of the Wolf: The Gospel in New Images.* The Seabury Press, 1970.

102. Carr, "The Children's Sermon: An Act of Worship." p. 20.

103. Ibid., p. 29ff., quoting McFague, *Speaking in Parables,* p. 41.

104. Ibid., p. 21.

105. Ibid., p. 20.

106. *Christian Worship: A Hymnal,* Special Edition. Christian Board of Publication, The Bethany Press, 1953. p. xxvi.

107. Horace T. Allen, Jr., *A Handbook for the Lectionary.* The Geneva Press, 1980. p. 197.

108. I. Howard Marshall, *Commentary on Luke,* The New International Greek Testament Commentary. William B. Eerdmans Publishing Company, 1978. pp. 716–717.

109. See, for example, Habakkuk 2:11 and Genesis 4:10.

110. One mistake I made was the use of paper bags as the means of distributing the gravel. Paper bags are too noisy and distracting for such a purpose. I would recommend using old offering plates or shallow pans with felt or paper on the inside to deaden the noise.

111. *Christian Worship: A Service Book.* Christian Board of Publication, The Bethany Press, 1958, ed. G. Edwin Osborn. p. 186.

112. Allen, *A Handbook for the Lectionary.* p. 183.

113. Ibid., p. 212.